The Female Tudor Scholar and Writer

The Female Tudor Scholar and Writer

The Life and Times of Margaret More Roper

Aimee Fleming

AN IMPRINT OF PEN & SWORD BOOKS LTD
YORKSHIRE – PHILADELPHIA

First published in Great Britain in 2024 by
Pen & Sword History
An imprint of
Pen & Sword Books Ltd
Yorkshire - Philadelphia

Copyright © Aimee Fleming, 2024

ISBN 978 1 39904 775 3

The right of Aimee Fleming to be identified as the Author of this work has been asserted by her in accordance with the Copyright, Designs and Patents Act 1988.

A CIP catalogue record for this book is available from the British Library.

All rights reserved. No part of this book may be reproduced or transmitted in any form or by any means, electronic or mechanical including photocopying, recording or by any information storage and retrieval system, without permission from the Publisher in writing.

Typeset in INDIA by IMPEC eSolutions
Printed and bound in the UK by CPI Group (UK) Ltd, Croydon, CR0 4YY

Pen & Sword Books Limited incorporates the imprints of Archaeology, Atlas, Aviation, Battleground, Digital, Discovery, Family History, Fiction, History, Local, Local History, Maritime, Military, Military Classics, Politics, Select, Transport, True Crime, After the Battle, Air World, Claymore Press, Frontline Publishing, Leo Cooper, Remember When, Seaforth Publishing, The Praetorian Press, Wharncliffe Books, Wharncliffe Local History, Wharncliffe Transport, Wharncliffe True Crime and White Owl.

For a complete list of Pen & Sword titles please contact:
PEN & SWORD BOOKS LIMITED
47 Church Street, Barnsley, South Yorkshire S70 2AS, United Kingdom
E-mail: enquiries@pen-and-sword.co.uk
Website: www.pen-and-sword.co.uk

or

PEN AND SWORD BOOKS
1950 Lawrence Road, Havertown, PA 19083, USA
E-mail: uspen-and-sword@casematepublishers.com
Website: www.penandswordbooks.com

Contents

Acknowledgements		vi
Preface		vii
Introduction		xii
Chapter 1	Early Life	1
Chapter 2	Life in the More Household	16
Chapter 3	Education and Adolescence	29
Chapter 4	Marriage and Writing	49
Chapter 5	Motherhood	69
Chapter 6	Humanism and Reputation	84
Chapter 7	Reformation	101
Chapter 8	Loyalty	116
Chapter 9	Mortality	134
Chapter 10	Legacy	147
Conclusion		158
Appendices		165
Bibliography		166
Endnotes		171
Index		181

Acknowledgements

I would like to take this opportunity to thank the following people, without whom I would not have completed this project. Firstly, to the staff at Pen and Sword, especially Amy Jordan, who had enough faith in me to say yes to my writing this book, and for all their help and advice. Thank you to my lovely editor, Gaynor Haliday, for her expertise and unending patience. Thank you also to Sue Palmer, the warden at St Dunstan's Church, for the warm welcome I was given and for sharing her knowledge of the church and Canterbury. Thanks to the wider history community for all their helpful hints, tips, and suggestions which helped me greatly.

An extra special thank you goes to my wonderful husband for his constant support, and to my children who patiently allowed me to work despite it making dinner late on more than one occasion.

Preface

Margaret More Roper and her family were arguably more well known by their contemporaries than they are in the present day. With a reputation of being well educated, and for their loyalty to their faith, the Mores were often used as an example of a modern, humanist household and to show the possibilities open to people who followed in their footsteps. Sir Thomas More was certainly an extraordinary man; he played a leading role in one of the most written about periods and was a trusted advisor to one of the most notorious English monarchs, King Henry VIII. His writings, his actions, his family life, and his eventual death and martyrdom for his beliefs have all led to him being a person of great interest to historians and he has been studied widely, with biographies about him and his role in these events available on most library shelves. It is thanks to the efforts of his daughter Margaret and the wider humanist movement, in preserving and publishing his works and letters, we know as much about him as we do – as an individual, and also about his thoughts and beliefs. And so, it is important that we understand Margaret if we are to understand her father, Sir Thomas More, as without her we would not have such a vivid picture of him, and equally, without his writings we may not have known very much about Margaret.

It is, however, difficult to separate Margaret from her father and wider household. Even when the subject at hand is Margaret, some historians and scholars have presented her merely as an extension of the story of her father. E.E. Reynolds in his biography of Margaret, written in 1960, said, 'This book may be regarded as a pendant to my Saint Thomas More [book], where many matters are treated in greater detail than would be justified in a life of his eldest daughter.'[1]

This 'justification' appears to have been that as a woman, and merely a daughter at that, she is neither the source, nor the subject. This echoes the early modern societal thought that as Thomas's eldest daughter, a woman in sixteenth-century England, she would not have been expected to have made much of an impression.

It is also true that the majority of the sources available to show us who Margaret was and what she did, thought or stood for, were recorded by those who were writing about or referring to her father, Thomas. The small number of pieces of evidence we have that belong to or are about Margaret exclusively are sparse and not particularly descriptive, and come from only a tiny number of individuals. We have only a small number of her works and only one surviving example of her handwriting. However, it is possible that by adding all these sources together we bring into view a woman who was extraordinary, in both her own time and also to our modern eyes.

Margaret's story is remarkable on many levels, the first of which is her gender. While her level of education and eloquence were not in of themselves unusual for a man in Tudor England, they were for a woman. Contemporaries of Margaret's, who did receive such an education, were almost exclusively nobility or part of the royal household. An example of this would be Princess Mary, eldest daughter of Henry VIII and Catherine of Aragon, who was given a broad education; experts were brought in from all over Europe to educate her. This was, however, due to her position, giving her 'princely skills' rather than those that would ordinarily have been expected for a woman. Queen Catherine herself was very well educated, again with a broad range of languages, scholarly skills and knowledge that allowed her to be able to hold her position as queen. The Spanish royal family gave all their children the same grounding; however, this was unusual for English queens prior to Catherine and it was her influence that led to Princess Mary being given a good education; this in turn makes Margaret's experience even more unusual. In Margaret's case it would not have been expected for her to have been educated to a level beyond what was necessary for a woman of her social status.

There were women who followed Margaret's path and, in the decades that followed, she and a small number of other prominent women, Queen Katherine Parr is one example, inspired others to achieve academic prowess with women's education being normalised in noble and royal households. This eventually filtered down through the strata of society; more and more women were given access to learning throughout the Tudor period and beyond. However, the More family's social status was not, in her early years at least, one that could be considered noble and therefore Margaret and her siblings' upbringing could and should be considered very unusual for her time period. In the early part of her life she and her family very much occupied the middle ranks of society: her father, mother and eventually her stepmother, all came from a certain amount of money and privilege, but not so much that they did not have to work for their positions and reputations. She and her brother and sisters, were, however, the beneficiaries of an extraordinary amount of experiences and were exposed to culture, thought and knowledge that would not be found in the average Tudor home.

It was her father's influence on their education that gave Margaret these opportunities to learn, but there was also an element of talent behind Margaret's work that again makes her stand out. She, like her father, was a gifted and enthusiastic scholar and with his guidance and the opportunities granted by his position and connections, she was able to grow and gain recognition for her abilities at a time when this was all but unheard of.

All these factors combine to make Margaret an interesting subject before we consider her own personal and religious achievements, the role she played in the events of the English Reformation, and her work on behalf of others. Margaret's life and work give us insights into the lives of some of the most prominent individuals in Tudor England and Early Modern Europe, and she has left a lasting legacy of source materials without which events of the period might never truly have been understood.

In this biography, my aim is to show just how important she was and how far her legacy has brought her. Considered extraordinary, even in her own lifetime, Margaret's life story gives us an example of what a woman, given opportunities, support and resources, could achieve in Early Modern England.

She is a vessel through which we can explore the events of those turbulent times of the Tudor dynasty, the reign of Henry VIII, and the English Reformation, examining it from a different perspective from those ordinarily seen. Using those events as a base we will see how Margaret was influenced by them, and how her life was shaped by the actions of those around her. I will examine the relationship between Margaret and Thomas closely, as this is important to give us context and information about them both, but I hope to bring out the parts most related to Margaret in particular so that we can attempt to get to know her as an individual: as a child, a daughter, a scholar, a wife and a mother, and as a woman who left such an indelible mark.

Introduction

1505

In a busy street in central London stands a tall brick house, set back from the hustle and bustle of the crowds and surrounded on both sides by shops and dwellings. Opposite is the imposing St Stephen's Church, and the River Thames runs so close you can smell its murky waters. There is noise and commotion from the barges being loaded and unloaded at the nearby docks, bringing goods from all over England, Europe, or even further. The Walbrook, a small stream that feeds into the Thames, trickles underfoot and you can hear it splashing under the little bridges and passages that straddle it. The unassuming building gives an impression of functionality, of frugality and of modest means, but inside a young couple are working hard to create a successful future for themselves in the cut-throat world of Tudor-era London.

Henry Tudor, King Henry VII, was on the throne. Having come to power by force at the Battle of Bosworth in 1485, a period of relative political stability almost verging on peace had settled over England. Aside from a small number who challenged him, Henry had established himself as a powerful and reliable monarch and with his wife, Elizabeth of York, had laid the foundations for a dynasty of Tudor kings and queens to come. The years following his accession had allowed London, and England generally, to blossom and grow into a metropolitan centre of culture and thought. Trade routes had opened up between English ports and Europe and the Middle East, and exploration of the New World would soon start to uncover its potential. As a result of the newly established stability and prosperity combined, England was also gaining favour and political influence.

This house described at the beginning was The Barge and it was the home of a young lawyer, Thomas More, and his wife Joanna, née Colt.[1] The couple had recently married, in January 1505. The More family and the Colt family were friendly with one another as a result of Sir John More, Thomas's father, who was a local politician in Cheapside and who served as Serjeant-at-Law for the district from 1503.[2] Sir John had a property at North Mimms, close to the Colt family home at Netherhall, Roydon in Essex. The Colt family had long been associated with the court, particularly during the reign of Edward IV for whom Thomas Colt, Joanna's grandfather, had been chancellor for a period of time. Both men were active in the legal world and their proximity outside of London would have been convenient to striking up a friendship. It was through this friendship that a 26-year-old Thomas More came to spend time with the Colt family and got to know both John Colt and his daughters.

Thomas – and perhaps other members of his family – went to stay with the Colts at Netherhall for the Christmas period of 1504, and he stayed for what appears to have been a reasonable amount of time. According to his son-in-law, Margaret's husband, William Roper, in his biography of Sir Thomas, Sir John Colt enjoyed Thomas's company and hoped that he would go on to marry one of his daughters:

Until he resorted to the house of one Master Colt, a gentleman of Essex, that had oft invited him thither, having three daughters, whose honest conversation and virtuous education provoked him there specially to set his affection.[3]

According to Roper, Thomas was initially considering marriage to the middle daughter, as 'he thought her the fairest and best favoured', but instead he opted for Joanna, who was the eldest, apparently out of pity and in order to not leave the eldest daughter overlooked for marriage. Apparently, to leave her in this situation would have caused issues and would 'be great grief and some shame … to the eldest to see her younger sister in marriage preferred before her'.

However, according to Desiderius Erasmus, who was an acquaintance and houseguest of the Mores (and who will prove to be an important source for much of our information regarding Margaret and the family as a whole), his choice of Joanna was not completely born out of pity. In his 1519 account he writes: '[Thomas] married a young girl of good family … choosing her, yet undeveloped, that he might more readily mould her to his tastes.'[4]

As such, Thomas could perhaps see that he could take Joanna as his bride, and by educating her and showing her by example, he would mould what he thought to be a suitable bride. Again, according to Erasmus, he taught her literature and music, and by doing so was attempting to make her into a 'charming life's companion'.

Their match was considered a good one and, even though Joanna was only 17 years old, in January 1505 she was wed to Thomas More who was almost ten years her senior. While there are no records of the marriage, it is likely that the ceremony took place at the parish church closest to Netherhall: St Peter ad Vincula in Roydon, Essex. Today, if you visit the village, you can see a picture of Thomas and Joanna on the village signs, alongside a depiction of Henry VIII who visited Netherhall with his infant son Edward, later Edward VI, *c*.1540.

The wedding would not have been as we know weddings today. Early sixteenth-century weddings were smaller ceremonies and, depending on the backgrounds of the bride and groom involved, could often be simple affairs with very few extravagances. The bride and groom would have met the priest at the doorway of the church and, with their invited guests looking on, they would have exchanged vows before entering the church as a married couple. There they would receive a blessing, and a Mass would be given to start their marriage. After the ceremony was complete, drinks of wine and beer would be served within the church to toast the couple and to signify the bond of kinship between the two families present. As with modern weddings, a ring would be given to the bride, but this was not a simple band. Instead it would have been whatever they saw fit, and could be extremely ornate if those involved could afford it. The bride would have worn her best dress for the occasion, but not the traditional white we see today, and the family would have been expected to do the same.[5] While for the majority (possibly with the exception of royalty and nobility) the occasion was a humble celebration, most would try to keep these traditions and, just as today, a wedding could become quite an expensive affair.

Following the ceremony and the drinks at the church, food would be served to the guests, usually at a nearby family home. In the case of the wedding of Joanna Colt to Thomas More, it can be assumed that the small wedding party would have enjoyed the blessing and drinks at the church in Roydon, and then would have returned to Netherhall for the wedding feast.

It was also customary for newlywed couples to stay in residence with their families, at least to begin with, so it is assumed that Thomas and Joanna would have returned to the More family home in Milk Street, Cheapside. Peter Ackroyd describes the area, in his biography of Sir Thomas More, as part of 'a fashionable and prosperous ward'.[6] John Stow, in his survey of London, first published in 1598, described the area as having 'many fair houses for wealthy merchants and other[s]'.[7] The More home, therefore, would have been a good place for the young couple to return to initially, especially given its proximity to the City of London and Thomas's work as a lawyer and in local politics with his father.

The family also had other members living nearby, which made it easier for them all to support one another as they tried to work their way upwards in society. Thomas's older sister, Joan, had married Richard Staverton, a lawyer training with Thomas at Lincoln's Inn. His younger sister Elizabeth, married John Rastell, who was a local politician, businessman and was involved in new technologies and advancements, including international trade and the new invention, the printing press. They all lived in the same areas of London, near to one another, and were a close family.[8]

It is not known exactly when they moved out of the Mores' on Milk Street and into The Barge at Bucklersbury, but it would appear the couple leased a small section of the building initially, later adding more on to their lease until eventually they had acquired the whole building for themselves.⁹ Stow describes The Barge as a 'great stone building ... manor or great house', Bucklersbury itself was, according to Ackroyd, 'a rather grand street' and was the area of the city that was populated by apothecaries and herbalists. As such, it had a reputation of being sweet smelling and refined compared to some areas. However, the proximity of the river and the Walbrook, which had once come right up to The Barge, and allowed ships to offload cargo there, meant that a sweet smell was not always guaranteed.¹⁰ The houses along the streets near Bucklersbury were also known for having large gardens and open spaces, and offered more room for a young family than the cramped streets of Cheapside. The house would be the family home for the Mores for the next twenty years and in that time they would make alterations and decorate repeatedly, to make this once industrial building into a comfortable residence.¹¹

The couple's move to The Barge meant that they would have a household of their own, as befitted their up-and-coming station. In 1504, Thomas had been made a member of parliament, representing Great Yarmouth. This work, alongside his legal work helping his father, who was still a Serjeant-at-Law and held a great deal of responsibility, meant that Thomas was starting to gain a reputation for being fastidious, with a good attention to detail, and had a promising career in front of him.

However, Thomas and Joanna were also focused on their personal lives, creating a home and starting a family, and in the autumn of 1505, the couple welcomed their first child, Margaret. We cannot be precisely sure of her exact date of birth, but we can deduce from portraits and other documents where her age is referenced, that she was born in the autumn, most probably the October. She was the first of four children, two more daughters, Elizabeth (b.1506) and Cecily (b.1507), and a son, John (b. *c.*1509/1510), who was most likely named for his grandfather. Unusually for the time, the quick succession of the births suggests that there were no other children, stillbirths or miscarriages. At this period, the infant mortality rate was precariously high, and there was little safety brought about by rank or privilege. One of the most well-known examples of the high infant mortality rate was the case of King Henry VIII and Queen Catherine of Aragon, who, despite conceiving six times in the first nine years of her marriage to Henry, only one child survived beyond infancy, and a further four were either born prematurely or stillborn. As a whole, statistically it has been shown that approximately 140 out of every 1,000 live births in the sixteenth century would end with the infant dying in its first year.[12] Leading on from this, approximately 330 out of every 1,000 would result in death before the age of 15. Diseases, even common childhood infections we take for granted today, would have been fatal, and cramped living conditions, lack of hygiene and poor nutrition all added to the high risk of a child dying, even in the most affluent of households. Statistics and evidence regarding stillbirths and miscarriages are very hard to account for, but midwifery and maternal healthcare was not commonplace and, as with childhood illnesses above, infections and lack of hygiene meant that childbearing and birth were extremely dangerous to both mother and child. However, luckily for the Mores, there appear to be no records of any problems in infancy and all the More siblings survived. For this particular family, the future appeared bright.

Chapter 1

Early Life

1509

The More family, with three young children and one more on the way, was very happily setting up a home in The Barge at Bucklersbury. Thomas was quietly getting on with his job as an MP, earning himself a reputation as a hard worker, and enjoying his role as a family man. Husband and wife were working together to bring about her education and to run a household, and things were looking very hopeful for the future; Margaret was almost 4 years old. However, in April 1509, Henry VII died and he left the throne to a 17-year-old Henry VIII. This marked the start of a great many changes for not only England and Europe but for the More family, especially Thomas.

As an MP, Thomas was expected to attend a great number of events after the king's death and, more prominently, the new king's coronation. His father, John More, was still serving as a Serjeant-at-Law and was an eminent man, influential in Cheapside, so when the coronation procession passed through the streets, he was one of the officials who made sure that the king and queen had the grandest of welcomes. The chronicler Edward Hall writes about the day, and describes it in detail:

> And the great part of the south side of Cheap, with cloth of gold ... And the streets railed and barred, on the one side, from over against Gracechurch, unto Bread Street, in Cheapside, where every occupation stood, in their liveries in order, beginning with base and mean occupations, and so ascending to the worshipful crafts: highest and lastly stood the mayor with the aldermen. The goldsmiths' stalls, unto the end of the Old Change, being replenished with Virgins in white, with branches of white wax: the priests and clerks, in rich copes, with crosses and censers of silver.[1]

As a part of the festivities, the dignitaries would have addressed the king and queen as they processed through, and John More, knowing Thomas's talents, had his son read a poem he had asked him to compose specifically for the occasion. This would have been a great honour and would undoubtedly have brought Thomas to the king's attention properly for the first time. He was already connected to the court both professionally and through friendships with clerics on the council, such as William Warham, the king's chancellor, but Thomas had yet to make an impression upon the king personally.

In the lengthy poem, Thomas describes the king as 'the glory of the era' and praises his rule copiously:

> But howsoever dutiful he was before, his crown
> has brought our prince a character which deserves to rule,
> Or he has provided promptly on his first day such
> advantages as few rulers have granted in extreme old age.[2]

This floridity of prose, combined with what was already a reputation for efficiency and his connections to court growing, show to us that Thomas was actively looking to ingratiate himself with the new monarch, and it appears to have paid off. In 1510, he was once again elected to sit in parliament, but this time as representative for one of the more influential boroughs of London; in that same year he became one of the two undersheriffs of the City of London. This meant that he was responsible for actioning the orders of the Mayor of London, and was required to attend events and represent the city. It was a sizable step up the career ladder for Thomas, and helped bolster his growing reputation for honesty and hard work in public service, developing even closer ties with the royal sphere and the bureaucracy that surrounded it.

As a result of this career progression, Thomas's position in politics and at court continued to improve, both in reputation and in pay, and this allowed the More family to have a relatively comfortable standard of living. In order to accommodate their growing family, the couple took on the lease for more and more of the building over the years; the house was large with rooms for guests, for storage and for Thomas to have a spacious study. It also had space for numerous servants, as well as large kitchens, stables and what John Guy describes as a 'summer parlour', a kind of conservatory or sunroom, which connected the main house with the considerable gardens.[3] There is evidence that they undertook decoration and works to adapt the house, to make it as comfortable as they could. Given the origins of the building as a weighhouse and storage warehouse, the house must have required a great deal of work to change the layout and to make it habitable as a family home. Guy even describes how 'a great tackle' hoisting mechanism was still present in the front courtyard even after the Mores had moved on from the property, showing just how industrial the building may have been when they took it on.

As well as all his work, home and family commitments, Thomas wrote consistently every day of his adult life, rising in the early hours to work; there was even a bed in his study which allowed him to sleep in his office and not be disturbed. This work ethic would be something that he would pass down to his children, and he had very high expectations of everyone in his household. Outside this work, however, he enjoyed time with his young family and Thomas was, despite his very busy schedule, responsibilities and the cultural expectations of the times, a hands-on father to his young children and was involved and invested in their upbringing.

Margaret's childhood experiences as a young girl in this period would have been pretty typical of a middle-class family in Tudor London. Young children were brought up together, in communal nursery arrangements until, at an age deemed appropriate – usually by the age of 7 – they would be separated by gender to receive their relevant education. For young children, very little was expected beyond basic skills and the ability to be polite, well spoken and well mannered. This type of practical education would have been left entirely on their mothers' shoulders.[4] A mother would also have to ensure that the children received their religious education from the family priest and they may have had basic instruction in reading, writing and perhaps a little music or language tuition, depending on the skills of their parents and caregivers. In the Mores' case, this would have been Joanna's responsibility, but judging by references to the children in Thomas's writings, he took an interest in the children's education from the outset.

Story-time would probably have been a key part for them, as you might expect with a father so keen on books and literature, and in their letters and accounts there are many references to Aesop's fables which it would appear was Thomas's influence. He recounts how he had enjoyed reading the tales with his own nursemaid as a child, and now he read the stories to his own children and they enjoyed them. Thomas would appear to have particularly liked them as they taught a moral lesson, and so had an educational purpose: 'There is almost no tale so foolish but that yet in one matter or other, to some purpose it may hap to serve.'[5]

The children would also have been encouraged to play and explore their surroundings. They may have had access to toys such as dolls, wooden items and even basic board games, but the More children were lucky; with access to a garden, they would have been able to play outside and with playmates so close in age, it is easy to imagine them playing together in those early years of their lives. Outdoor space was something of a luxury for children growing up in the crowded city.

Their gardens at The Barge contained fruit trees, arbours for shade and even an aviary filled with birds. Thomas enjoyed keeping animals in general and, as Guy lists, the family also had chickens in a coop behind the kitchens, as well as rabbits, dogs and even in later years a pet monkey![6] This pet monkey can be seen in the family portraits painted by Holbein, in the lower right-hand corner of the painting, seated next to Dame Alice. The many animals and pets give an insight into the family home that Margaret would have known as a young child, the fun that was present there and the love that she felt for her father.

The family were enjoying the fruits of Thomas's labours in their large house, gardens and beautiful surroundings, and, despite his growing responsibilities from 1510 onwards taking him away from home more frequently, the family appeared to be going from strength to strength, but this rosy outlook for the More family was about to change catastrophically. In the summer of 1511, the family found themselves dramatically wrenched from their idyllic bubble when, completely unexpectedly, Joanna More passed away. She was still only 24 years old and she left behind her husband and their four very young children.

It is unclear how she died or if there was a specific cause such as an illness. There appears to be two prevailing theories: either a complication from childbearing or birth, or a sickness that appears in some other accounts from the time. It is uncertain what the illness was. Some have identified it as an outbreak of the sweating sickness but, as Guy and others point out, the outbreaks of 1506 and 1507 are well reported as being the sweat, with the next recorded epidemic not showing until 1518.[7]

The sweating sickness was much feared in the early modern period; prayers for protection from the disease were written to be spoken all across the country and even though it was some time after the last severe cases were reported, the fear still remained in the public consciousness. Shakespeare mentions it as late as 1604 when this line appears in *Measure for Measure*: 'Thus, what with the war, what with the sweat, what with the gallows, and what with poverty …'.

It would strike quickly, with very little warning, was highly contagious and, in a very high number of cases, was fatal. The symptoms were dizziness, headaches and general malaise that, within hours, would turn into a burning fever, extreme sweating and delirium. The physician John Caius, who was an English physician and experienced a later outbreak in 1551, concluded that death would normally occur between three and eighteen hours of the first onset of symptoms, but if the person afflicted survived for twenty-four hours, they would more than likely survive.[8] Sweating sickness, often referred to as 'the sweats', 'stop-gallant' (as it was associated with affecting the upper classes of society), or simply the sickness or plague, was present mainly in England from its first recorded cases in 1485 until it dwindled after the outbreak of 1551. It was thought by Caius to have been airborne, caused by the filth and lack of clean air in England's towns and cities. It mainly affected middle-aged people, with very few children or elderly people falling victim to it, although there were some. There have been theories regarding how the sickness began and how it spread, and even today it is unclear what type of illness caused the sweating sickness. What is known is that in years when the sweat hit, the mortality rate of those affected could be as high as 50 per cent.[9] In the outbreak of 1485, the disease claimed approximately 15,000 lives in London alone.[10]

The illness that struck London in 1511 was much more likely to have been a variant of influenza, or an outbreak of typhus or dysentery. Most summers, the nobles that inhabited the palaces and houses of the cities would leave the built-up areas and head into the country to avoid the illnesses that inevitably broke out among the populace of dirty and cramped cities; the more humble and those who were required to stay would have no choice but to risk catching whatever ailment was working its way through the population.

Equally, the cause of Joanna's death, as theorised by historians, could have been to do with the birth of another child. John, their youngest child was born in late 1509 or early 1510 and given that all the children were born in swift succession, it is likely that Joanna could have been pregnant again in the summer of 1511.[11] However, in the many letters we have from Thomas, and also from visitors to the house from the time, nothing is mentioned about either a pregnancy, the loss of a child, or anything related to another child being expected. This is unusual, as even in early modern times, and certainly for a devoted father like Thomas, a new baby would at the very least have been noteworthy.

Joanna's death, whatever the cause, was definitely a shock to the whole family, and it seems likely that the family were concerned that she had died from a contagious or dangerous illness as she was buried very shortly after her death, at the church of St Stephen Walbrook. This was their family church, just across the street from The Barge, and was where the children had been baptised.

Unlike today, deaths and funerals were not a particularly private affair, and the community would come together to mourn a loss. A bell would be rung to announce a death in the parish, and also just before a funeral to let anyone in the vicinity know it was happening so they could come and pay their respects to the dead. Death was a common occurrence, but even so if someone died at a relatively young age, having survived childhood and appearing to be healthy, it was still a shock to everyone who knew them. If someone was popular, or, like Joanna, they lived in a built-up area with a high population, it is likely that the bereaved family would have been joined by many mourners.

The death of Joanna would have impacted everyone in the house instantly. The children, including a 5-year-old Margaret, would have witnessed their mother's body being bound in a shroud and covered in sweet-smelling herbs and oils, and then laid on a bier – a board or stretcher to be carried – in the family home on the night before the service. The whole family would have accompanied Joanna's body on its final short journey to the church, and even though they were all very young, they also would all have attended the full service to see their mother's body blessed and lowered into the grave, which was most likely within the church building itself, under the flagstones.

As the eldest child, Margaret would also have been expected to say a prayer for her mother's soul as a part of the funeral service, known as the offertory. Guy describes the prayer as having been 'for her mother's everlasting joy and salvation' and Catholic funeral services today have a prayer that may well be similar to the words Margaret would have recited:

> O God, who hast commanded us to honour our father and our mother;
> in Thy mercy have pity on the soul of my mother,
> and forgive her her trespasses;
> and make me to see her again in the joy of everlasting brightness.[12]

For Margaret, a tiny girl of 5 standing in front of a packed congregation to say these words must have been terrifying. It does, however, show us her strength of character and also why, in years to come, she was so strongly connected to her father, with whom she must have felt united through their shared grief. As grief-stricken as he may have been though, Thomas shocked everyone who knew him by moving on with his life incredibly swiftly and, little more than a month after Joanna's death, he was once again married to an acquaintance of the family, Alice Middleton.

Alice was a member of the Arden family, who owned estates in Essex and whose neighbours were the Colts. She was distantly related to the royal Tudor dynasty through Owen Tudor, great-grandfather of Henry VIII, and her father had held the same post as Thomas's father, as a Serjeant-at-Law. She was four years older than Thomas, and brought with her lands and money from her previous marriage to John Middleton, a wealthy and reasonably successful merchant. Thomas and John Middleton moved in similar circles, were members of some of the same companies and groups, which is how he first became aware of Alice and knew of her character. The Mores and the Middletons also lived and socialised in similar areas and circles; John Middleton's businesses were based in and around Fenchurch Street, around half a mile from Cheapside and Milk Street where John More and the extended More family had lived, and the More estates at North Mimms were not far from other lands owned by John Middleton in Hertfordshire. The two families may well have been very familiar with one another.[13]

John Middleton died in 1509 leaving Alice a widow of 34, pregnant and with two daughters to provide for. Unfortunately,

Alice miscarried the baby, and her younger daughter, Helen, died from illness not long after. This left Alice and her daughter, also called Alice and aged around 10, alone. When Joanna More died in 1511, Alice was 36 years old and it was entirely possible that she might go on to have more children and this, combined with the inheritance from her marriage, meant that Alice was certainly eligible and with good prospects for remarriage, and Thomas wasted no time in proposing.[14]

Thomas and Alice's hasty marriage in 1511 did cause a bit of a stir though. In order to be married, the couple had to apply for a dispensation from the reading of the banns, which customarily would have been on three consecutive Sundays in the church where the ceremony was to take place, as well as other parish churches where they each may have worshipped. This particular ceremony took place at St Stephen Walbrook, and we learn about the speed of events from the priest who performed the wedding, John Bouge, who later in his life wrote about his experiences with Thomas More:

> He was my parishioner at London. I christened him two goodly children. I buried his first wife, and within a month after, he came to me on a Sunday at night late, and there he brought me a dispensation to be married the next Monday without any banns asking ... [15]

With both Thomas and Alice being on their own with young children to support and raise, their marriage, according to Erasmus, was 'more for the care of his children than for his own pleasure'.[16] It was thought to be 'going against friends' advice and common custom' to marry so quickly and with so little sentiment, and Reynolds describes the marriage as a 'cool-headed arrangement'.[17] However, Erasmus goes on to say that '[Thomas's] life with her is as blithe and sweet as if she had all the attractiveness of youth, and with his buoyant gaiety he wins her to more compliance than severity could command.' Their union allowed for mutual benefit and support; both Alice and Thomas now had stable parent figures for their young children and their relatively successful social and financial positions, as well as Thomas's ability to continue to pursue his professional goals, were stabilised further through the marriage. Not only that, Erasmus's thoughts show that despite the inauspicious and functional nature of their arrangements in the beginning, the Mores' marriage appears to have been a relatively happy and comfortable one.

Accounts from the time show that Alice definitely ran a tight ship and, in some cases, this may have rubbed people up the wrong way. Andrea Ammonio, Henry VIII's Latin secretary and a houseguest of the Mores on a number of occasions, wrote about Alice and Joanna and seems to have preferred Joanna. He describes Joanna in more positive tones, as 'his (Thomas More's) gentle wife', who when he wrote to Erasmus 'never thinks of you without a kind wish'. This is in stark contrast to his description of Alice. In another letter to Erasmus he recounts:

> I have moved at last to St Thomas's College, where I am more housed according to my ideas than I was with More. I do not see the hooked beak of the harpy, but there are many other things that offend me, so that I really do not know how I can still go on living in England.

Ammonio had been staying with the Mores from Christmas 1510 until this letter was written in the autumn of 1511. He had been with them for the death of Joanna, and then for More's remarriage, but then appears to have left abruptly when Alice moved into The Barge. We do not know whether Ammonio was asked to leave, was forced out by clashing personalities, or moved on due to circumstances outside of his relationship with the Mores, but his comments about Alice are not particularly flattering, suggesting they did not get on well. Erasmus too had cut short one of his visits to the More home due to feeling he had outstayed his welcome in Alice's eyes.[18] However, we should be cautious when judging Alice purely on the descriptions of these two men, both of whom have a reputation for being awkward and may not have been the most obliging of houseguests for their host. Erasmus in particular is often described as a particularly awkward houseguest who, as an example, refused to speak or even to learn any English, despite his prolonged stays in England, and as the family spoke no Dutch, he and Thomas would converse purely in Latin, leaving the rest of the family out of their conversations. He did not dance, or eat certain foods in fear that his health would be affected, and often complained about pains in many different parts of his body.[19] Ammonio's comment about there being 'many other things that offend me, so that I really do not know how I can still go on living in England', should perhaps make us cautious about his version of events, and of using them to judge Alice's character.[20]

Indeed, Thomas himself seems to have very much enjoyed Alice's company. On the tomb which Thomas had constructed in 1532 for his first wife at their parish church in Chelsea, the intention in the inscription appears to have been that Alice would also be buried there when the time came. The inscription reads:

> Here lies Johannas, the dear little wife of Thomas More who intends this tomb for Alice and himself. The first, united to me in my youthful years, gave me a boy and three girls to call me father. The second – a rare quality in a stepmother – was as affectionate as if her step children were her own. It is hard to say if the first lived with me more beloved that the second does now. O how blessed if fate and religion had permitted us all three to live together. I pray the tomb and heaven may unite us; thus death will give what life could not.[21]

The merger of the two families happened quickly though, and the arrival of a whole new step and extended family, so soon after the death of their mother, would surely have been deeply unsettling for the young More children. Margaret would have been around 6 years of age when the family took up residence together at The Barge. By the end of 1511, Thomas, his family life once again stable with his new wife ably running his household and his professional life calling him away from home more than ever before, was establishing himself as a trustworthy lawyer, scholar and an academic. He was making friendships and connections with humanists all over Europe, and his connections with the court were gaining momentum. In 1510 we can see evidence of this career success, as Thomas joined the Christmas celebrations at court and was elected as 'Lord of Misrule'. This role meant that he became, for that one feast at least, the most important man at court, and this role was usually given to a rising star or court favourite. However, this would have meant him spending long periods away from the family home at a time when he would normally have wanted to be with his beloved children.[22]

Another clue about his rising reputation was that Thomas was also writing all the more frequently to Erasmus and other eminent scholars and becoming well known to many around him. Despite the heartache and sorrows that accompanied the death of Joanna, for the More family all this attention meant that their star was in the ascendant.

Chapter 2

Life in the More Household

1511

The More family household had merged with the Middleton family, which meant that there were now five children, all aged 10 and under, in the nursery. They were not the only children in the household, however, as alongside the More and Middleton children, there were also other children living with them: wards, fostered children and others who would join the household for their education.

The first of these was Margaret Giggs, who was taken in by Thomas and Joanna as an infant. She was the daughter of a neighbour of the Mores, Thomas Giggs, who was a mercer, or tradesman, in the city. When Joanna gave birth to Margaret, his wife (referred to in records only as 'Mistress Giggs') had also recently given birth herself and it seems likely that Mistress Giggs had also been wet nurse to Margaret More when she was a baby.[1] It was quite usual for mothers of wealthier households, who wished to conceive again, to employ women to act as wet nurses to their infants for anything up to a year. The baby would often be housed with the wet nurse and as the Giggs family lived very close to The Barge, this would have been a very convenient arrangement. When Mistress Giggs died suddenly in 1506/1507, soon after returning Margaret to the More household and their nursery, the Mores adopted Margaret Giggs and raised her alongside their own children.

Margaret was not the only ward that the Mores took on; in fact, she was the first of many. In 1524, Thomas was involved in the hearing of the case of the lands of Edward Cresacre, of Barnburgh, a small village near Doncaster in South Yorkshire. This case came under what were termed 'poor men's causes' and Thomas, alongside Thomas Wolsey and other officials, including the king, oversaw these cases personally. Edward Cresacre had died leaving his lands and monies to his wife. His only heir was his infant daughter, Anne.[2] Cresacre's widow remarried and her new husband, Ralph Rokeby, conspired to marry the infant Anne to his own son, John, who was himself only a child. When they were only 6 years old he, completely illegally, put the two children in front of a priest and demanded they were married. The local magistrate, Sir Robert Constable, took action to stop the marriage of the children, but he himself had his eye on the Cresacre inheritance and, when Anne was still only 12, had her betrothed to his son, who took advantage and raped the girl.[3]

All this drama was brought to a head when Constable was brought before the Star Chamber, fined 1,000 marks (a mark was two-thirds of a pound, so this was the equivalent of £666) and he was made to apologise to the king for his actions. He was granted a pardon and released, with responsibility for Anne going forward being given to Thomas and Alice More. She was welcomed into the Mores' home and became part of the family, very quickly settling into their ways and routines.

There were many others who came into the More home, many as impressionable teenagers looking to learn from Thomas, or to study at Lincoln's Inn just as he had done. William Roper, Giles Heron, Thomas Elrington and William Dauncey were names that appear in the correspondence and were living with the Mores for a time. All of them either had links to the family, or to Alice's family, and came to them with good recommendations from others about their character and willingness to learn. Some were betrothed to Thomas's daughters and came to live in the family home to start their marriage, as was the tradition. Others, such as William Roper, came for the education and obviously made a good impression as they were allowed to stay and marry one of the More daughters or wards.

As well as wards and adopted children, the Mores played host to a number of others who joined the household as lodgers, as tutors to the children, or a little of both. Thomas, during his travels earlier in his career, had formed close friendships with like-minded academics and reformers and, thanks to his work at court, the family frequently entertained diplomats, courtiers and scholars from across Europe, some of them staying for prolonged periods of time. Some of this was reciprocal for times that Thomas had been abroad and had stayed with families in a similar way. In his younger years, he had travelled widely in Europe, particularly in France, Belgium and the Netherlands, and the scholars who came to him were often from these same places, sent by his acquaintances on recommendation, or simply visiting him, as was the case for Erasmus, as they were close friends. As a result of these visits, Thomas and his entire family were exposed to a wide range of subjects, topics of discussion and beliefs. As Peter Ackroyd describes, 'the Old Barge had developed into a scholarly household in the spirit of, if not upon the same scale as, the academies of Italy,' and this demonstrates well just how much scholarly discussion, and just how many well-respected men entered the More house and were connected with the family.[4]

Some of these visitors, such as Andrea Ammonio and Erasmus, stayed with the family for a long time, and became a part of the household on a day-to-day level while they were staying with them; they were also to form close bonds with the family members and be intertwined with their futures. Most of those who came into the More house were connected in some way to the extended family, or to Thomas's work which took him all over Europe, but when they did stay with the Mores they were all expected to be fully involved in the daily routines of the household.

The family would all rise early, but none so early as Thomas, who would wake at dawn to pray and then to write before the rest of the working day. Breakfast and morning prayers would be attended by all members of the household, and the same for evening meals, where a passage would be read from the Bible by one member of the household, and then discussed over the course of the meal. While the children were young and in the nursery, meals would have been an adult affair, but once their education had begun in earnest, all members of the household, be they family or visitors, would be encouraged to participate in the mealtime readings and discussions, and to engage others at the table in conversation. Thomas would often work late into the day, but the family would eat and carry on with their discussions, even in his absence, and he would leave suggestions for passages for them to read, or topics for them to explore during their dinnertime debates. If Thomas was working in his study, with his assistants and clerks often spending all their time in the house as a result, then he would lead the debates himself and ensure everyone present had full understanding of the topics discussed.[5]

The almost constant flow of visitors, lodgers, clerks and scholars, and the mere presence of at least five children in the house at any one time, meant that the More family home was a hive of activity and everyone in the house had their roles to play. While Thomas attended his roles at court, or secreted himself into his study, the children would have a full day of lessons and activities, and also would be expected to help their stepmother with the care for the animals and with everyday tasks around the home.

The Mores were not what could be considered rich, but they were also far from poor and employed a small staff to run the house: a cook to provide meals, housekeepers and maids to clean, wash and help to serve meals. While the children were still in a nursery, the maids would have helped with looking after the children. Infants stayed with their wet nurse until they were about a year old, after which they would return to the house full-time; the wet nurse may have lived in the house for that time, or, as in the case of Mistress Giggs, they may have lived close by and been able to bring the infant to the family home regularly. Other members of the 'service' may have included a 'house boy' to fetch and carry for the cook or housekeepers, run errands and make deliveries. Thomas would also have had a personal 'gentleman' to see to his needs – who would have slept either at the foot of his bed or directly outside the door on a small cot, so as to be on hand should he be required – and a secretary to help with some of his bureaucratic works. Some of the time, the role of secretary was fulfilled by some of those who came to stay with the Mores and was viewed in the same vein as an apprenticeship. In later years, John Wood became his principal gentleman and was an integral and trusted part of the household, particularly supporting Thomas with his work.

Changes to Thomas's career path after the ascension of Henry VIII meant that the family started to enjoy greater privilege and, to a certain extent, wealth. As time progressed, they added items including wall hangings and rugs, to furnish their rooms more comfortably, and took on more lands and buildings at The Barge, all of which would have required improvements to bring them up to the same level of comfort as the rest of the house. This expansion of both space and means in turn allowed for visitors to become more frequent.

Even before his marriage to Joanna in 1505, Thomas had struck up a friendship with Desiderius Erasmus, the noted theologian and scholar. He began his career as a Catholic priest, and wrote extensively about the Catholic Church and its ways of worship. His work made him a controversial figure, and put him and those who were in agreement with him, such as Thomas, into a group known as Humanists. Thomas had stayed with him on a few occasions when he travelled to Europe, and had corresponded with him regularly since their first meeting. While staying with Erasmus, Thomas had been inspired to write his work *Utopia* which was eventually published in 1516 to much acclaim. The two men would talk about theology, politics and the Classics, and found each other good company.

In 1499, Erasmus had come to England to study and to take up positions as a tutor at Oxford University, and to be housed by William Blount, Baron Mountjoy, as his patron. Mountjoy was a scholar himself, and had stayed with Erasmus in Paris in 1497, and had learned a great deal from him during his stay and so was keen to reciprocate when Erasmus came to England. In 1498, upon his return from Paris, Mountjoy was appointed Prince Henry's 'companion at studies' and was to form his education around the aim of making him a new Renaissance prince. Erasmus was a friend to Mountjoy and greatly admired him, writing:

> Lord Mountjoy swept me away ... where indeed would I not follow a young man so enlightened, so kindly and so amiable? I would follow him, as God loves me, even to the lower world itself.[6]

Through this friendship, Thomas and Erasmus, along with a small group of other law students from Lincoln's Inn, were invited to visit the royal children's home and nursery at Eltham Palace in Kent. There they would meet with the children of Henry VII and Elizabeth of York, among them an 8-year-old Prince Henry, the future Henry VIII. The prince made an impression on the men and, even though Erasmus remembered the prince's age wrongly, he did record events of the day:

> I was staying at lord Mountjoy's country house when Thomas More came to see me, and took me out with him for a walk as far as the next village, where all the king's children except prince Arthur ... were being educated. When we came into the hall, the attendants not only of the palace but

also of Mountjoy's household were all assembled. In the midst stood prince Henry, then nine years old, and having already something of royalty in his demeanour, in which there was a certain dignity combined with singular courtesy. More ... presented [Henry] with some writing. For my part, not having expected anything of the sort, I had nothing to offer, but promised that on another occasion I would in some way declare my duty towards him. Meanwhile I was angry with More for not having warned me, especially as the boy sent me a little note, while we were at dinner, to challenge something from my pen. I went home, and in the Muses' spite, from whom I had been so long divorced, finished the poem within three days.[7]

Erasmus did not, however, receive any response to his work.

Thomas at this point was still a student and very much up and coming in his reputation but, as Peter Ackroyd notes, his connections to the royal household and his apparent position of trust would suggest he was a familiar face to Mountjoy, and also respected in his character. Ackroyd elaborates:

It was surely unusual for a young law student to be allowed access to the royal family of England, and to be on terms of such familiarity that he might bring a companion apparently unannounced.[8]

Access to the royal school room and the Renaissance-inspired education of the young royals, particularly focused on Prince Henry in this case, was something that would be considered an honour, and perhaps it was Thomas's friendship with Mountjoy that allowed this to happen, and, with Mountjoy also being a follower of the Humanist movement, this friendship may have inspired and influenced Thomas's own thoughts about education when it came to his own children later on.

While Thomas's Humanist connections continued to grow thanks to his friendships at court, such as that with Mountjoy, his career went from strength to strength and his friendship with Erasmus was one that would remain close and endure. The two men continued to write to each other prolifically and they visited one another whenever they were able to do so. In 1506, Erasmus once again came to England and this time stayed with the Mores at The Barge for a number of weeks. In 1509, he returned again, ostensibly to attend the celebrations for the coronation of Henry VIII, but in the end he stayed with the family for a year or more. The children were only small, Margaret herself merely 4 years old, so the austere man who had moved in with them, spoke no English and spent so much time in their father's study, taking him away from them, must have been an intimidating presence in the house, and a challenge for their mother. If Thomas had to leave, Erasmus would stay in the house and, well known for his complaints about his health, he would complain about aggravated kidney stones, the lack of his books and belongings and generally be 'awkward, restless and unsociable'.[9]

Despite all this, it was while staying at The Barge that he composed 'In Praise of Folly', or *Moriae Encomium*: 'With nothing to do, I began to amuse myself with a eulogy of folly. I had no idea of publication but [wrote it] simply as a distraction from the pain of my complaint.'[10]

The work was a satirical essay picking fault with the superstitions and corrupt practices associated with society, but particularly with the Catholic Church. When it was printed in 1511, the work was very popular amongst reformist and humanist communities. Erasmus dedicated the work to Thomas, making him out to be the inspiration for the work and as the embodiment of what a true friend and Christian should be:

> Among these you, my More, came first in my mind, whose memory, though absent yourself, gives me such delight in my absence, as when present with you I ever found in your company; than which, let me perish if in all my life I ever met with anything more delectable. And therefore, being satisfied that something was to be done, and that that time was no wise proper for any serious matter, I resolved to make some sport with the praise of folly … Finally, if anyone is still unappeased by all I have said, he should at least remember that there is merit in being attacked by Folly, for when I made her the narrator I had to maintain her character in appropriate style. But why do I say all this to you, an advocate without peer for giving your best service to causes even when they are not the best? Farewell, learned More; be a stout champion to your namesake Folly.[11]

The correlation of More and 'Morae' in the title, and the joint translation from the Greek and Latin of 'Morae' as both 'More' and 'Folly', was a source of great amusement for both men, and both of them enjoyed the popularity and notoriety that the work gained. Erasmus wrote: 'I let some close friends have a look at what I'd done, so as to add to my amusement by sharing the joke.'[12]

In the summer of 1510, after a year living at The Barge, Erasmus moved on from London to Cambridge to take up a teaching position there, and then he returned once again to Bucklersbury to join the family for their Christmas celebrations. This would have been at the request of Joanna as much as Thomas, as the festivities would have been organised by her. Christmas festivities in this period were a longer affair than we have now, lasting from Christmas Eve until Twelfth Night on 6 January. The whole period was full of frivolity and feasting and with Thomas doing so well, the house would have been full of food and music, and guests would have been a welcome addition to the celebrations. As much as it would have pleased Thomas to have his friend with them for the festivities, his role as 'Lord of Misrule' took him away from home on the important days, and away from his family and good friend, leaving Joanna and the children to play host.

Her generosity as a hostess is shown more by the fact that Erasmus brought with him Andrea Ammonio, whom Guy describes as 'an opinionated Italian said to have the manners of a prize fighter and the appetite of a horse'. Despite Erasmus leaving promptly after Twelfth Night to return to Cambridge, Ammonio stayed on at The Barge well after the festive period was over and for months going into the summer and autumn of 1511. His letters to Erasmus provide us with a great deal of insight into the household. Of Joanna he writes that: '[More's] most agreeable wife [is] extremely well' and that she 'never mentions you [Erasmus] without blessing your name'.[13]

Ammonio was still a guest in this home when Joanna died suddenly, and he was a witness to the turbulent events that surrounded her death and Thomas's swift remarriage to Alice Middleton. Unlike Joanna though, Alice was not as happy to play hostess to Erasmus and other visitors to the Barge; Guy details how she thought of them as "no better than scroungers and time-wasters' and they were equally indifferent to her.[14] Indeed Erasmus, having been such as regular visitor to the More home, actively avoided the place now that Alice was in charge, describing her as 'capable and vigilant', but the true two-facedness of this description is lost somewhat in translation. Ammonio was unceremoniously cast out following the marriage and he called her 'blunt and rude' in return. He was moved to alternative accommodation where, even though Thomas attempted to make his stay there comfortable, he was left unhappy – which appears to have been his way.

These visitors were not the last or only ones to come to stay with the More family. As Thomas's career advanced, more people joined the family for periods and when they did, they too were welcomed into the family for meals and took part in their prayers and celebrations. The More children would, therefore, be in direct contact with these visitors and as a result some of them made quite an impression upon them, and would become instrumental in their lives. Some of the visitors would even take on some of the children's education. When Thomas was called away from the family home, which began to happen more and more frequently, he would entrust everything to do with the home and the children to Alice, who enlisted their small loyal staff of servants, and to a number of tutors and lodgers who would form the extended household. As the adoption of Margaret Giggs shows, a close bond formed between the family and those who made up the household. The Mores became more than a family of five, they were a tight-knit community who shared ideals, discussed ideas and challenged one another.

Margaret's experience of the house in these early days would have been one of a constantly changing sea of faces, of different people who spoke many languages and who took up much of her beloved father's time and energy, but who would ask questions and talk to her and tell her stories of their homelands and of their own childhoods. Margaret and her siblings would have been too young to really grasp who these people were and why they were important to their father, or to society in general, but their presence could have acted as a catalyst for their natural curiosity for experiences, learning and the wider world. For Margaret and her sisters and brother, this allowed for a much broader set of horizons than would normally be afforded a child in this period, let alone for girls like her.

Chapter 3

Education and Adolescence

1512

Margaret was about 6 years old when her father married Alice Middleton and their family expanded with new members of the household. With the arrival of Alice's daughter, who was a little older than Margaret, into the sibling group, and also Margaret Giggs, of a similar age to the More children, Thomas and Alice strove to give the children the very best education they possibly could.

Children in this period would spend their first few years in a communal nursery. There was very little in the way of formal learning, and boys and girls were treated almost identically, even wearing similar clothing and playing games together.[1] Formal tuition and academic learning would begin usually at around 7 or 8 years of age and continue until the child was 14 or 15 years old, when they would progress on to the next stage of their lives.

In the majority of cases, formal education and scholarly learning in the fifteenth and sixteenth centuries was the reserve of male children in the middle and upper echelons of society. They would receive tutelage in languages, philosophy and theology and be encouraged to pursue other interests such as music, sports or military exercises such as swordsmanship, archery and even the joust.[2] These were generally accepted as the courtly skills a male child would need in order to pursue any lucrative and sought-after careers. In middle- and upper-class households, away from the nobility, the law or the clergy were often seen as pathways to bettering one's social status. Families with connections could send their teenaged boys, and sometimes girls, to be educated in households with other children. The young Prince Henry was educated with a number of contemporaries with whom he remained great friends throughout his life, Francis Bryan and Charles Brandon among them. These boys were sent to the royal household to benefit from the education while forming friendships and connections that could possibly help them in later life.

Learning and education would usually take place in the home under the supervision of tutors or parents, although, especially in cities, many boys attended schools. These schools were often attached to churches, cathedrals or monasteries, or were run by charitable groups to help raise the standards of living for the young in the cities and towns. Thomas More had received such an education, as an example, attending St Anthony's School on Threadneedle Street, close to his family home in Cheapside.[3] The school was one of the finest grammar schools in London at the time, attached to St Anthony's Church and hospital, which provided care and almshouses for the poor of the local area. St Anthony's was a 'free school', which meant that boys from all over the parish were able to attend, while other contemporary schools charged up to 16d a week for lessons, excluding all but the wealthier local residents from attending. While there, Thomas would first have learned to read and to write in English, and then progressed to learning Latin. The school was a 'grammar' school, meaning it focused on the Latin language and all lessons, writings and even conversations would be expected to take place in Latin, especially for the older boys. William Roper, in his later biography of his father-in-law, describes Thomas's school days and the times afterwards:

> after he had been brought up in the Latin tongue at St Anthony's in London – was by his father's procurement received into the house of the right reverend, wise and learned prelate, Cardinal Moreton ... In whose wit and towardness the Cardinal much delighting would often say of him unto the nobles that divers times dined with him 'this child here waiting at the table whosoever shall live to see it, will prove a marvellous man.' Whereupon, for his better furtherance in learning, he placed him at Oxford, where, when he was both in the Greek and Latin tongue put to an Inn of Chancery.
>
> From thence was admitted to Lincoln's Inn, with a very small allowance, continuing there his study until he was made accounted a worthy utter barrister.[4]

In Thomas's own example we can see the type of education that a boy could receive and where that education would potentially take them if they were able and had the right connections. Boys would stay in these schools or with their tutors until they reached an acceptable age and were advanced enough in skills and then they would move on to take up apprenticeships, more specialist training or even, for some, university. Education provided boys with the ability to climb the social ladder by training in professions such as law, accountancy, local government roles or training for the priesthood, and it opened doors for those who were able to take advantage of opportunities which arose.

For girls, however, there were far lower expectations. Unlike their male siblings, they were not automatically given access to the same scholarly subjects or to any other professional training opportunities. Throughout the early modern period and beyond, it was very unusual for women to be given formal schooling at all, and when they did it was often done at an individual level, and was often costly. Formal education was not accessible for the masses until the nineteenth century, and it was not until the Education Act of 1880 that it was made compulsory that all children, be they boys or girls, attend primary education up to the age of 11. Secondary provision did not become a formal requirement for all children, including girls, until the twentieth century.

There was, however, an appetite for girls to be educated before this and the first recognised girls' school to offer formal education to girls in England was opened in London 1850 by Frances Buss. The school, The North London Collegiate School, is still open today as a private girls-only school.

Going even further than that, the first women to enter the university system in Britain did not do so until 1869, when 'The Edinburgh Seven' became the first women to achieve a degree when they all qualified in medicine. For law, the arrival of women into the university system took even longer, and the first woman to achieve a law degree was Eliza Orme in 1888. Women's education, therefore, took many centuries to reach a level of equality of access to that of men. Early modern women were not expected to reach anywhere near the educational or professional levels of their modern descendants.

Instead, in early modern society, education for girls was seen as helping girls to prepare for the roles they would be expected to perform in their adult lives: becoming mothers, heads of households, and the wives of gentlemen. This all required a skillset involving some knowledge of languages and some household management skills. Alison Sim puts this nicely when she says in her book, *The Tudor Housewife*: 'A woman's vocation was above all to see that her husband was comfortable, that his children were fed, clothed, disciplined and educated and that his servants behaved themselves and worked hard.'[5] Knowledge of scholarly subjects such as classics was not usually included in preparation for this role and was instead replaced with music, dancing, needlework and other genteel pursuits, which were all encouraged and supposed to show up their lady-like qualities. Education was, in the words of Kate Aughterson, purely for 'the cultivation of virtue and the development of the skills of housewifery'.[6]

Girls from middle classes and levels of society would sometimes be shown a trade or have a small amount of training in a family business. This would enable them to help with the business and aid in the running of the business if their husbands were to go out of town or were ill and unable to work. However, this was almost always informal and was not necessarily something that would be promoted. A woman's place was considered to always be subservient to a man, and therefore a woman would not be presented as equally knowledgeable or to appear to be his superior in any way.

Reading and writing though were considered essential skills, needed to keep books, send correspondence and to keep good order through careful management of staff and assets; many gentlemen were landlords or owned multiple interests and investments and if they were away at court or on business it would fall on their wives to deal with issues that may arise in their absence. However, the reading and writing that a woman was expected to be able to do was constrained by moral guidelines and the expectations outlined above: chastity, faithfulness, godliness, motherhood and generally being a good wife and companion. In *The Christen State of Matrimonye*, written by Heinrich Bullinger in 1541, he outlines that parents should educate their daughters to avoid:

> unhonest daunsynge, wanton communicacion, coommary with rybaldes and fthy speeches. Teache them to averte thyr sight and senses from all such inconveniences, let them avoid yollenes, be occupied wither doing some profitable thyng for your family, or elles readynge some godly booke. Let them not reade bokes of fables, of fond lyght love, but call upon God to have pure hartes and chaste, that they might cleave only to thyr spouse.[7]

Girls from rural families were often sent to bigger, more cosmopolitan households, to broaden their experiences, and give them practice of courtly manners and behaviours. Some, more affluent, families would even manage to gain invitations to send their daughters to serve at the court of foreign nobility, giving them experiences that they potentially could not have had if they had stayed in England. Becoming fluent in foreign languages and learning customs of other cultures would possibly serve aristocratic wives well should their husbands be invited to be diplomats, or if they had to entertain foreign dignitaries. Famously, this was the case for Anne Boleyn, who spent time as a young girl at the service of first Margaret of Austria, and then as a lady-in-waiting to Queen Claude of France.[8] The experience would also, for the benefit of the family as a whole, bring their daughters to the attention of many possible suitors and allow for more favourable marriages to be made, particularly when a family was ambitious.

Thomas More's attitude towards the education of girls was far from usual for the period, indeed for the mediaeval and early modern world in general, and seemed to differ from that which we have explored in this chapter so far. From the very beginning of his adult life, he set out to find himself a wife who was a companion and in Joanna he thought he had someone who, in Erasmus's words, he could: 'readily mould her to his tastes. He had her taught literature, and trained her in every kind of music; and she was just growing into a charming life's companion for him when she died.'[9]

His remarriage, to Alice, also saw him looking for an educated companion. Again, we learn from Erasmus that Alice, whom he describes as 'middle aged, set in her ways, and much occupied with her home', following her marriage to Thomas learned 'to sing to the lyre and the lute, the monochord or the flute, and to do a daily task fixed by her husband'.[10]

What these daily tasks were is unclear; however, they may have been in line with what More himself regarded as essential learning, and which would enable Alice to competently educate their children.

This need for his wives to have a level of education was not purely a selfish one. He said, 'a woman should be well educated in order to be a guide in her children's education and an erudite conversationalist for her husband, who would gladly desert male companionship for her company.'[11]

In his epigram, written c.1516, More sets out to persuade his contemporaries on the benefits of marrying a woman who is 'either educated or capable of being educated': 'Education is of great benefit to women themselves because it gives them an invaluable tool for achieving greater closeness with God.'[12]

This epigram appears to support the humanist belief that in order for a woman, for a wife and a mother, to provide her children with a good and pious upbringing, she herself must have the knowledge and the skills gained from such an education and in so doing the husband and wife will create a home that is entirely closer to God. More attempts to present the educated woman, a woman of eloquence and learning, in a positive light. He shows examples of learned women from antiquity to show how women's education is not a threat to men's position, but instead could be of great benefit to the entire household.

There was, however, debate, even amongst humanists about the depth and breadth that should make up this education. As a mother was only really supposed to be responsible for the spiritual side of her children's learning, some, including Juan Luis Vives, in his work *De Institutione foeminae Christianae* or *The Education of a Christian Woman* published in 1523, omitted classical scholarship; languages such as Latin and Greek were discouraged and 'difficult' subjects such as mathematics were omitted altogether from his programme of study.[13] Instead, Vives focuses on the conduct of the woman and the virtues as a woman in support of her husband and father, and never to surpass them in any way. This follows on from more traditional views, following the classical work of Aristotle, that women were 'the animal inferior to man', and therefore would not be capable of learning to the same levels as their male counterparts. There was worry amongst contemporaries of More that allowing a girl to be educated might endanger her virtue and teaching her good as well as evil deeds, instead of allowing her to decipher between the two, would lead a woman astray due to inherent frailty of character, embodied by Eve in the Bible.

Vives was a Spanish scholar who had stayed with the Mores briefly before writing his work. The book was dedicated to Catherine of Aragon, queen of England at the time of its publication, and was later translated into other languages including, in 1529, into English by Richard Hyrde, whom we shall get to know better later in Margaret's story. The book became influential all over Europe and had a bearing on the education of many women of the period, including Queen Catherine's daughter, Princess Mary. The content of the book was considered radical by some contemporaries; he lists pages of learned women whom he deems to be good and virtuous, lists books that should be read, and those that should be avoided, and states that all girls should be educated for the good of their soul.[14] We must remember though that Mary was born in 1516, when Margaret was 11 years old, and she and her siblings had already begun receiving their education at the hands of their father and his chosen tutors, at what came to be known informally as the 'More School'. By the time Vives published his book in 1523, Thomas had been a proponent of the very ideas that he was talking about for more than a decade, and the educational reputation of the More household was firmly established. Perhaps Vives' stay with the Mores had been inspirational to him, and had allowed him to formulate the ideas for his own work.

From 1511/1512, following the arrival of Alice and the upheaval that brought with it, it became important for the family to begin to move forward, and this meant the start of education for the three eldest girls in the household: Alice Middleton, Margaret Giggs and Margaret More. They would eventually be joined by their younger siblings as they grew old enough to take part in lessons, and all would be taught together, to a lesson plan designed by their father according to what he believed to be important for their futures.

Thomas took a keen interest in his children's education and well-being. In his biography, Thomas Stapleton says:

> We must now speak of More as a parent and describe, as well as we can, how he employed his great gifts in the education of his children. We may be sure that he ever acted as befitted a scholar and saint. His first care was the religious training of his children; second only to his zeal for their advancement in learning ... As soon, then, as his children were old enough to begin their education, he taught them personally or by a tutor.[15]

His career and his writing continued to take him away from his home and family regularly, which was not something that Thomas liked at all. William Roper tells us that when he was away from his family he 'Began somewhat to dissemble his nature, and so by little and little from his former mirth to disuse himself'.[16]

Whether this was tactical in order to make himself into an unattractive companion to the king and court, or whether he genuinely felt low when he was apart from his family is unclear, although in a later letter to Margaret he does say that he 'would make a sacrifice of wealth, and bid adieu to other cares and business, to attend to my children and family'.[17]

However, despite his feelings on the matter Thomas was away frequently, and often for prolonged periods and this meant that he had to employ tutors to school his children in his absence. These tutors were usually men who were involved in the humanist movement, or who came to the More home through Thomas's work, and therefore Thomas felt that they were suitable candidates to instruct his children according to his wishes. Thomas was still very involved in the education of his children, even when absent, writing letters to the children and to their tutors regularly and commenting on pieces of work or letters that they had sent. This set-up is what is sometimes referred to as the 'More School'. Erasmus first coined the phrase, stating that '[Thomas More's] house was a school for the knowledge and practice of the Christian faith,' and it came to be used to describe More's home and educational setting for his children, and also the type and style of formalised education that the children were given.[18]

Some of these tutors employed by Thomas were well known in their own rights before tutoring the More children, or would go on to make their own impacts in the scholarly world. They included John Clement, who was probably a recommendation of Thomas's friend William Lilly. Clement had been a student of Lilly's, and is referred to in letters as early as 1515. Around 1518, he transferred to the household of Cardinal Wolsey and was replaced by William Gonnell. Gonnell was originally from just outside of Cambridge, where it would appear that he had come to know and do some work with Erasmus while he was teaching there. He came to the Mores in 1518 and appears to have stayed at least until 1521 when, in a letter to his children, Thomas refers to 'Master Drew' and 'Master Nicholas' as being tutors to the children. 'Master Nicholas' refers to Nicholas Kratzer, who was at the time of the letter astronomer to Henry VIII and so would have been at court with Thomas More. Also recorded is Richard Hyrde, who in his introduction to his translation of Juan Luis Vives' *The Education of a Christian Woman* refers to Thomas as 'my singular good master and bringer-up'. While it is not certain whether he was full-time tutor to the children, or if he was more of an ad-hoc teacher, he appears in records from 1521 onwards, up until his death in 1528.[19] Thomas refers in his letters to the 'many and excellent' tutors who were instructing his children, so it is reasonable to assume that there were many more involved in some way in the education of the children. Also clear is the role that Alice played in ensuring that the children completed their studies and that Thomas's letters, tasks and other wishes were carried out even in his absence.

Thomas had very specific ideas about how his children, including his daughters and the girls under his care, would be educated. Unusually he chose to provide access to all subjects and types of education to his daughters, despite popular opinion of the time and the thoughts of his contemporaries being predominantly that girls either couldn't or shouldn't have this kind of learning. This conflict of opinion was one that Thomas was keenly aware of, and even included in correspondence to their tutor William Gonnell, when giving him instruction on how and what to teach to the children:

> Since erudition in women is a new thing and a reproach to the indolence of men, many will gladly attack it, and impute to scholarship what is really the fault of nature, thinking to get their own ignorance esteemed as a virtue by contrast with the vices of the learned.[20]

Later in the same letter he continues:

> If it be true that the soil of a woman's brain be bad, and more likely to bear bracken than corn (and on this account many keep women from study), I think, on the contrary, that on the same grounds a women's wit is to be cultivated all the more diligently, so that nature's defect may be redressed by industry.[21]

Their curriculum included subjects that, as previously mentioned, would not have featured at all in a girl's education previously. Subjects such as Latin and Greek were generally dismissed as unnecessary and mathematics, biological sciences and astronomy were all omitted, but all these and more were taught to the More children and in great detail. Particular emphasis on the Latin and Greek allowed Thomas to teach his children from the classics directly, and they learned to hone their language skills through reading and eventually, translation. In a letter home to the children, praising them for their diligent hard work, Thomas writes:

> Did I not love you so warmly I should really envy your good fortune in that so many excellent tutors have fallen to your lot. But I think you no longer need Master Nicholas as you have learned whatever he had to teach you in astronomy. I hear you are so far advanced in that science that you can point out the pole-star or the dog star or any of the constellations.[22]

Such a varied and challenging curriculum may well be considered to be a tough challenge for any child, but it would appear that the More children, in particular Margaret, were entirely capable of meeting it. Some of the children appear to have had more talent for some subjects than others, for example there are references to Margaret Giggs having an 'algorism stone' for use in mathematics, but the same skills were taught to all the children, and they all appeared to thrive in the environment. Thomas himself also set a staggeringly hard-working example for the rest of his 'school' to follow by writing every day, praying multiple times daily, producing fine literary works, all while working on his legal caseload and gaining more and more responsibility within the king's court. This attitude of hard work being its own reward, and the children seeing for themselves what can be achieved through intellect and perseverance, was a powerful lesson for the children to follow. Their father's published works also would have been available for them to read, and as they grew older and were more able to understand them, and also understand the mechanisms of the printing press and its ability to spread word and influence, Margaret in particular seems to have really taken up her father's writing baton. She showed aptitude for languages, for Latin and Greek, for translation, and for interpretation of text and deductive reasoning. Thomas would set the children work to be completed, such as to consider the murder mystery in the declamation of Quintillian, and it was work like this that bonded father and daughter through the written word.

As a result of all this work done by Thomas and the children, and the interactions the children had with their tutors and visitors such as Erasmus, the More house started to gather something of a reputation as a house of learning and scholarly pursuits, and the children themselves became well known for their acumen and their dedication to their learning. Vives in his dedication praises the Mores directly and by name, stating:

> Now if a man may be suffered among queens to speak of more mean folk, I would reckon among this sort the daughters of Sir Thomas More, Knight – Margaret, Elizabeth, Cecilia and with them their kinswoman, Margaret Giggs – whom their father not content only to have them good and very chaste, would also they should be well learned, supposing that by that means they should be more truly and surely chaste.[23]

Thomas's opinions and his fervent enthusiasm for the egalitarian education of his children was controversial but it was influential and following his example other writers took up the cause of the education of young women. This included the works previously mentioned of Juan Luis Vives, and later Roger Ascham's work *The Scholemaster*, which was printed posthumously in 1570, on his experience as tutor to the future Queen Elizabeth I. While it was unusual, Thomas was not alone in his beliefs and, following the reputation built on his model of the More School, and other examples from the continent, other families began to educate their children. Mary I, Elizabeth I, Katherine Parr, the Grey family including Lady Jane, and the daughters of Anthony Cooke, who became tutor to Edward VI, were all educated to a higher level than ladies in previous generations, and would all influence yet more women both directly and indirectly.

Some of the reputation and influence that the family and its school may have come from Thomas's prolific letter writing, and his propensity to boast about his children to all who would listen. The family were separated frequently and for reasonably long periods of time due to Thomas's work at court. He was often called to go abroad, or to travel with the court on progress, but they were a very close family unit and Thomas continued to be involved in the education of his children even over great distances. As a part of this he encouraged his children to write to him frequently, and:

> Now I expect from each of you a letter almost every day. I will not admit excuses ... such as want of time, sudden departure of the letter-carrier, or want of something to write about. No one hinders you from writing but, on the contrary, all are urging you to do it ... How can a subject

be wanting when you write to me, since I am glad to hear of your studies or of your games, and you will please me most if, when there is nothing to write about, you write about that nothing at great length.[24]

The letters that Thomas wrote give us an insight into the relationships between him, his children and more specifically, with Margaret. As one of the eldest in the household Margaret was soon able to correspond with her father at length, and tell him the daily goings on in the house, as well as to correspond with him about more academic topics that she was studying. Though unfortunately none of her early letters to her father survive, we do have a number of his responses to her, and these give a picture of a loving daughter writing to her father, who then responds in the warmest terms, while still reminding her of the importance of her studies almost constantly:

> I was delighted to receive your letter, my dearest Margaret, informing me of Shaw's condition. I should have still been more delighted if you had told me of the studies you and your brother are engaged in, of your daily reading, your pleasant discussions ... For although everything you write gives me pleasure, yet the most exquisite delight of all comes from reading what none but you and your brother could have written.[25]

We see through the letters also that, as Margaret grew older and her skills and abilities began to show through, she appears to take on a new role in Thomas's life; as a confidant, and as his pupil rather than simply his daughter. She is referred to in the letter shown above as being of equal stature to her brother, John, whom it appears through other letters, was more keen to write to his father in comparison to the other children; according to his description they may have taken a more slapdash approach to their correspondence. In Thomas's letter to his 'Dearest Children' he writes:

> There was not one of your letters that did not please me extremely; but to confess frankly what I feel, the letter of my son John pleased me best, both because it was longer than the others, and because he seems to have given to it more labour and study.[26]

In the same letter he chastises the children for not caring about presentation, content, and of not correcting their translations of their letters into Latin thoroughly enough. It would appear that while being a loving and caring father, Thomas was a taskmaster and would have made Margaret and the rest of her siblings work hard for the praise that they received. He also refers to the girls as 'chatterboxes' who should have no trouble finding what to say in a letter, as they 'have always a world to say about nothing at all'.

Margaret's letters were, however, the ones that Thomas chose to share with others while he travelled around Europe. In very early 1521, when Margaret would have been just 15 years old, he wrote to her to tell her of the impression that her letter gave to Reginald Pole, at that point still resident in England and welcome in court:

I cannot put down on paper, indeed I can hardly express in my own mind the deep pleasure that I received from you very well-expressed letter, my dearest Margaret. As I read it there was with me a young man of the noblest rank ... Reginald Pole. He thought your letter nothing short of miraculous. ... I could scarce make him believe that you had not been helped by a master until I told him in all good faith that there was no such master at our house, nor would it be possible to find any such man who would not need your help in composing letters rather than be able to give any assistance to you.[27]

Erasmus also talks about Thomas sending him examples, or having the children correspond directly with him, as an exercise for them but also to show his good friend their 'progress in learning' as he called it in his letter to his friend Guillaume Budé:

He told them all to write to me, each without any help, nor did he suggest the subject nor make any corrections ... Believe me my dear Budé, I never was more surprised; there was nothing whatever either silly or girlish in what they said and the style was such that you could feel they were making daily progress.[28]

The letters, and the responses made by her father, also show vividly the fondness that he had for her. He consistently refers to Margaret as 'my dearest Margaret' and when addressing the letters to the whole school, he often singles her out for mention or for more specific questions than were put to her siblings. At this point though, all the More siblings are mentioned in equal measure by sources such as Erasmus and Vives, all the children appearing notable for their academic achievements within the school and under the supervision of their father.

The foundations were laid in this period for Margaret, alongside her brother and sisters, to become more and more well known throughout England and further afield. She had shown through her work that she had the acumen and the ability to achieve great things and had also cemented herself in the affections of her father for just these qualities. As Margaret entered adulthood and took on her own responsibilities, her world, and her influence upon it, would continue to change and grow.

Chapter 4

Marriage and Writing

1520

In the year 1520, Margaret turned 15. For both she, and the rest of the More family, the next few years were to bring big changes and the first of these was to affect Margaret the most directly; her marriage.

For young women in the early Tudor period it was common for marriages to take place at any time from around 12 years of age. This was the minimum age that was required and in some royal families there would be contractual betrothal ceremonies prior to the age of 12 to formally recognise a future union. However, the further down society you look, the older the two people actually getting married would statistically get. Studies show that from 1566–1619, a little after Margaret's time but still within the same period, the average age to be married was 27 years.[1] According to the authors of the studies, some of this could be explained by those getting married waiting until they were able to set up their own homes before they got married, or simply a lack of urgency on the part of the families of working people in marrying children off, and losing the income and labour that was provided by that family member to the family pot.

Marriage was not always a romantic endeavour in the early modern period either. Marriages, especially to those with family assets and inheritance to worry about, were often more about linking families together, making lucrative arrangements and ensuring the security of their holdings for future generations. It is rare that a couple would 'marry for love' unless they were either very lucky, or were not at the mercy of family wealth or instruction to guide their decision making.

In Margaret's case, however, and also in the case of most of her siblings, marriage was entered into young, and was for the most part, to bind the family together with others who were connected to them.

Margaret's stepsister, Alice Middleton, was the first to get married when in 1516 at the age of 15 she married Thomas Elrington. Thomas Elrington was an heir to an estate in Essex and may possibly have been linked once again to the Colt family. Their marriage appears to have been a relatively happy one, with the couple staying with the Mores at Bucklersbury for periods and so that Alice could continue her education. Their first child arrived in 1520, who was christened Thomas. This was the first of three children, and the first of many grandchildren for Thomas More and Alice to dote upon.

With Alice's marriage at such a young age, she set the precedent for Margaret to expect to be married at around that age, and so, when Margaret turned 15 it would have triggered the start of negotiations to make the best match possible. Thomas More was by then an MP and doing well, but was still not considered of high status or of particularly great power or influence. As such, a modest match was made with William Roper.

Roper was the eldest son of John Roper, a lawyer who went on to become the Attorney General to Henry VIII, and a long-time friend of John More, Thomas More's father. The Roper family had land in Kent at both Eltham and in Canterbury, and had long been a noble family in the county. When William chose to follow in his father's footsteps and study law at Lincoln's Inn, he joined the More household to study and to learn from Thomas More, in a sort of apprentice role. It is thought he joined the household in 1518, when he was about 22 years old, and Margaret was 13.

Erasmus described William Roper as a young man 'who is wealthy, of excellent and modest character and not unacquainted with literature'.[2] His education and his lineage made him a good candidate for marriage to their Margaret, and for the Ropers the match was one that cemented their long-standing friendships and put their son in the same circles as the Mores who, through the work of both Thomas and his father, Sir John, were in the ascendent.

Margaret More and William Roper married in July 1521, most likely at St Stephen's, their family parish church at Bucklersbury. The same church where, ten years earlier, her mother had been buried, and where the whole family attended services every week. Unlike the wedding of her mother and father, it is likely that their wedding would have been well attended. Family members, members of the More and Roper households, and perhaps even dignitaries from the court and from Lincoln's Inn, would have been in attendance and partaken in drinks and food offered by the wedding party, and the bells would have rung out of the church tower in celebration. The church itself had seen so many More family events that it must have seemed like familiar ground for Margaret and maybe this would have helped the young girl to get through the ceremony and all that it meant.

Following their wedding the pair were given a small house in Eltham, close to the Roper family residence of Well Hall. However, due to their young ages and William still being in tutelage at Lincoln's Inn, the newly-weds continued to live with the More family at Bucklersbury. While they were there Margaret and William were still actively part of the family and both were encouraged to continue to study in the 'school', and to continue as they had done before their marriage. Margaret continued to write to her father, and carry on with translations just as she had done before her wedding, and she and William carried on being members of the household.

In the years to come all the remaining More children would be married also. In 1525 both Elizabeth and Cecily were married; Elizabeth to William Dauncey, a privy councillor to Henry VIII, and Cecily to Giles Heron, a member of parliament. Shortly after this, in 1526, Margaret Giggs married John Clement, the children's former tutor who had gone on to become physician to the king. Margaret was 21 when they married, and perhaps because of her age and also John Clement's position at court, the couple set up home at The Barge at Bucklersbury, which had now been vacated after the More family had moved out to their new estate home at Chelsea. Thomas More still held the lease for The Barge, and so the Clements were still very much a part of the Mores' extended household and family. Lastly, John More, the youngest More sibling, married Anne Cresacre, the Mores' ward, in 1528. They were 19 and 18 years old respectively and one has to wonder whether, as the two youngest and the last two of the More School remaining without a partner, they chose to marry one another to remain together.[3]

Around the time that Margaret and William were married in 1521, Thomas More received a number of accolades which helped to bolster his position at court. He was made under-treasurer of the Exchequer, working under Cardinal Wolsey, the Lord Chancellor, and earning £173 a year. As was the custom for the under-treasurer, he also became Sir Thomas More. Henry VIII wrote that he was now 'our trusty and wel beloved counsellor Thomas Moore, now knight'.[4] This role entailed secretarial work in the closest circles of court to the king, and as such he became closer to King Henry and his influence grew as he was asked more frequently for his advice on matters ranging from foreign policy to domestic taxation. Shortly after this increase in his rank, in 1523 Sir Thomas became MP and 'Knight of the Shire' for Middlesex and from this was elected as the speaker of the House of Commons, a position that came to him on Wolsey's own recommendation. In 1525 another promotion came when he was made chancellor of the Duchy of Lancaster, which made him responsible for much of the North of England. He was now established as one of the most influential men at court and was one of King Henry's most trusted officials.

Thanks to the increasingly important role that Sir Thomas was playing, it was a busy time for all the More family. The marriages of the children, the arrival of grandchildren, and the need to constantly entertain and work on court proceedings from his home, meant that Thomas and his family were increasingly living in cramped quarters at The Barge. It was a large home, and the extensions of their lease to include more of the building made it even more so as time went on. However, with his position now as it was, there came with it certain expectations. Their home in Bucklersbury was no longer fit for purpose as the home of such a politician, and as such, in *c.*1522, around the time of his promotion within court and his change in situation, Sir Thomas took out the lease on a portion of land in Chelsea.

Chelsea, in comparison to The Barge, was a domain. To reach it took hours by river or road, covering a distance of 4 miles to the palaces at Westminster and Greenwich, 6 miles from the Tower of London and, in the other direction, 18 miles from the palace of Cardinal Wolsey at Hampton Court. However, this isolation suited Sir Thomas well, as he was able to retreat from the hustle and bustle of the city to his family and his books in the relative calm of rural Chelsea. The land he leased covered a large area including grounds and gardens that, once the house was built in *c.*1523, were landscaped and allowed the Mores to keep their menagerie along with more formal gardens for walking in and entertaining guests.[5] Famously the house played host to many dignitaries and even the king, Henry VIII, would stop by to speak to More and to enjoy the hospitality offered by his friend and advisor.

The house itself was large, almost verging on palatial. It had grand dining halls and balconies overlooking them, as well as suites of rooms for the family and those who lodged with them. There was even an adjacent smaller house, known as the New Building, later referred to as Butts Close, which also had bedrooms, studies, a small chapel and all the same features of the larger house, but on a smaller scale. William Roper describes it in his biography:

And because he was desirous for godly purposed sometime to be solitary, and sequester himself from worldly company, a good distance from the mansion house builded he a place call the New Building, wherein there was a chapel, a library and a gallery. In which, as his use was upon other days to occupy himself in prayer and study together, so on the Friday there usually continued he from morning till evening, spending his time only in devout prayers and spiritual exercises.[6]

It appears then that this house was designed by Sir Thomas to give himself a smaller retreat in which to study, write and contemplate, away from the busy main house which by this point was full of people including a lot of small children. Erasmus, who incidentally never actually visited the Mores at Chelsea, writing in 1532, describes the home of his friend in a letter to an acquaintance John Faber, the Bishop of Vienna. In the letter he speaks of just how many people were living in the Mores' home at the time:

> More had built himself on the banks of the Thames not far from London, a country house that is dignified and adequate without being so magnificent as to excite envy. Here he lives happily with his family, consisting of his wife, his son and daughter in law, three daughters with their husbands and already eleven grandchildren. It would be difficult to find a man more fond of children than he.[7]

To Sir Thomas and the whole of the More family, including Margaret, the study of the Christian faith was key, as it always had been, to the Mores' household routine, and the house even had a large private chapel for the family to use for private prayer. However, for the most part they chose as a family to worship at the parish church, known as Chelsea Old Church. The church was located not far from their new home and was a magnificent example of a medieval church. It was here that the family would pray whenever they could, and despite Sir Thomas's ever increasing rank and status, they continued to do so throughout their time in Chelsea.

Despite all the upheavals and changes of this period, Margaret and her siblings alongside the other members of the 'school' continued with their learning and programme of studies that was drawn up for them by their father. It is probable that Richard Hyrde, their tutor from 1521 onwards, went with them to Chelsea, and would have taught William Roper, and became a close friend of them both. By this time Margaret's skills were starting to outpace any teacher though, and the tutors that were in the house to tutor her siblings, and then their children, were more like equals rather than mentors. In the letter from February 1521, where we learn how impressed Reginald Pole was by her writings, Thomas is very clear that 'nor would it be possible to find any such man who would not need your help in composing letters rather than be able to give any assistance to you'.[8] Margaret's skills had grown, and this was despite challenges, and he writes how Pole was impressed 'even before he understood how you were pressed for time and distracted by ill health, whilst you managed to write so long a letter'.

Alongside her skills and obvious talents for the written word, Margaret's own personal opinions were also beginning to become defined in this period. Her father's involvement in the Humanist movement spilled over into the household, and would have been a subject that was talked about at length amongst the family members and, as she got older, Margaret began to concentrate on studying works that were popular within the movement, scriptures and classical works from philosophers, as well as more contemporary writing. Her work became more ambitious in its nature, and she was influenced to greater and greater extents by the works of her father and others within his humanist circles.

In 1523, Erasmus published his *Precatio Dominica*, a study of the Lord's Prayer and how a good Christian could learn from it. This was written in Latin, and was, alongside his translations of the Testaments and his other works about the church, a part of his growing catalogue of humanist writings. In 1524, just one year later, Margaret Roper published her English translation of this piece, and Richard Hyrde wrote the introduction on her behalf. The title page doesn't name Margaret overtly; however, references made to the author do not make it difficult to identify her:

> A devout treatise upon the Paternoster made fyrst in latyn by the moost famous doctour mayster Erasmus Roterodamus and tourned into englisshe by a young vertuous and well lerned gentylwoman of nineteen yere of age.[9]

Margaret's own identity is kept anonymous, and there was a lengthy introduction written by Richard Hyrde in which he describes the 'lerned gentylwoman' a little deeper but her identity is not given explicitly. But, as More's daughters had a reputation for their learning, both Hyrde and Erasmus had well established and widely known connections to them, and the age of the woman is given, it is clear to most readers but most especially to those in the humanist community, that the translator is in fact Margaret.

The publication made ripples in all directions as was the first piece by a non-royal woman to be printed and widely distributed in England. Previously Margaret Beaufort had been the only person who had done so, and her work had been in Latin.[10] Margaret More's work in English was the first of its kind to be printed, and by doing so, she was opening herself up to criticism and attack, as well as bringing into question the works of Erasmus and her father. Women's education, as has been discussed before, was controversial; it was considered not to be necessary by most, and even dangerous by some. In translating and then publishing her work, Margaret was not only making a statement about herself, but was highlighting the whole question of the place of women in society.

Translation in and of itself was not a controversial activity for women. For some, including prominent figures such as Margaret Beaufort and others in Europe such as Christine de Pisan who were held up as examples of how a woman could be 'learned', it was a means to get closer to and to gain deeper understanding of written works, particularly scripture. Translating passages of the Bible was a common practice amongst women, particularly when they wished to demonstrate their piety, and to use their time in a productive, Christian manner. Richard Hyrde wrote in detail about how translation kept the mind busy to avoid the temptation of idleness, either of the mind or the body:

> Redyng and studying of bokes so occupied the mynde
> that it can have no leyser to muse of delyte in other fantasies
> whan in all handy werkes
> that men saye be more mete for a woman
> the body may be busy in one place
> and the mynde walking in another
> and while they syt sowing and spinnying with their fyngers
> maye caste and copasse many pevysshe fantasies in their myndes
> which must nedes be occupied
> outher with good or badde
> so long as they be wakynge.[11]

Doing so for a profit, however, made the act of translating into something completely different; it could be considered vain or greedy to do so for money or for reputation, both of which were deeply undesirable and unbecoming qualities and ran contrary to the pious nature of the act of translation in the first place. The women who had done so in the past had very much done so with outward the aim of spreading inspiration of faith and of deepening their own relationship with God, and as the translations had been done before the invention of the printing press they hadn't been able to be distributed widely. This caveat of 'godliness' and as a public show of piety had, for the most part, softened any criticisms of the women involved or their intentions.[12] However, now, Margaret's piece of work was printed and distributed widely and had the potential to show her as a vain, un-pious woman, and this is why her name was kept off the cover, even though the clues left there meant that most did not even have to guess that it was her work. For her reputation to be protected, however, this illusion of privacy and, therefore, of modesty, had to be maintained. Even the cover image of a young woman who is meant to represent this 'lerned gentylwoman', studious and quiet, appears to try to allay fears about women's learning and involvement in religion. It shows a woman in a study, in a home and the surroundings, clothes and the face are demure and lacking in any frivolity. She is shown as literally the image of piety, of modesty and of the domestic.[13]

Translation was also something that Thomas often asked his daughters to do. Indeed he would have them write their own letters out in English, then Latin, then translate back into English to ensure their use of language was correct and meaning was not lost. They would translate passages of their father's works also, and parts of the classics to show they fully understood its working and meaning. In learning languages it is a common practice educationally, and so it was something that all would be familiar with. However, there were some issues with Margaret's choice to translate, and then publish, texts by Erasmus.[14]

As we have already established, there was a bond between the Mores, Margaret and Desiderius Erasmus, that stretched back to her childhood. In correspondence she refers to him as 'her teacher', and while he never would have actually taught Margaret formally, his works, his advice and his influence on Thomas, would undoubtedly have meant that she would have been completely familiar with him, and have a deep affection for him as a family friend. When Margaret chose to translate Erasmus's work on the Lord's prayer, however, she was entering an argument that surrounded him as a scholar and this brought her work into the spotlight of closer scrutiny.

Erasmus was considered radical, and despite his protestations to the contrary, many thought him to be sympathetic to Martin Luther. In 1517 Luther had written his *95 Theses* and in doing so he had started the process of the reformation of the Christian church. Erasmus himself had been highly critical of the church, calling for reform and for a return to scripture as the root of all worship, *Sola Scriptura*. Martin Luther had been influenced by this criticism of the church, and his *95 Theses* pointed out many of the same points that Erasmus had highlighted in his writings, and he was therefore linked to the work that Luther was doing on the continent by proxy. His works were also being printed and distributed alongside other Protestant works, such as Tyndale's English Bible and Luther's pamphlets.[15]

In 1524, when Margaret chose to translate the *Precatio Dominica* into English, Erasmus' work was, therefore, being viewed with great suspicion by the authorities and Cardinal Wolsey had banned all domestic printing, and imports from abroad, of his works as well as a whole host of other related literature. If found in possession of these prints, a person could be accused of heresy. Writing of religious texts in English had been branded heretical since John Wyclif had translated the Bible into English in the late fourteenth century and this translation had been adopted by a group known as the Lollards. The Lollards had rejected the papacy and called for a return to scripture alone, but they had also become linked with rebellion and some of the instigators of the Peasant's Revolt of 1381 had tried to use it to push forward their ideas. At this point, Lollardy,

English Bibles and all criticism of church authority was seen as heretical, treasonous, and banned completely in all forms. This was over a century before Erasmus and Luther were writing, but the legacy of these events still remained and caused those who followed Erasmus, or Luther, or wrote about these things in English, to be tarred with the same brush.

It is therefore striking that Margaret chose this particular piece to not only translate in private, but also to publish into the public sphere. Even though it is possible that the writing has a deep personal connection and significance, she risked bringing herself and her family, including her father who was rising rapidly through the ranks at court, into disrepute. Not only that, but she risked being arrested and put on trial for heresy for which the punishments ranged from simple imprisonment, through to burning at the stake. There is an argument amongst historians that Margaret's translation hadn't just been an academic act, but that perhaps using Margaret as a conduit to bring these works back into England was a carefully thought out plan. It could be considered that Humanists wanted to enable their thoughts and policies to be distributed to a wider audience, and by making use of the reputation of Margaret and the rest of her household as good pious Christians, Erasmus and his writings could by association be shown to be non-heretical and, in fact, supportive of the Catholic faith and church.[16]

Whatever Margaret's reasons for doing so, she worked hard on translating what was a lengthy and detailed piece of writing. The *Devout Treatise upon the Paternoster* consists of seven petitions, or chapters, each one dealing with a specific part of the Lord's prayer and how to interpret it.[17] The work looks to give deeper understanding of the use of the words that were spoken by Jesus when he recited the Lord's Prayer. Here is the very beginning, where 'Abba Pater' or 'Our Father' is discussed in detail:

> Abba pater whiche in Englysshe is as moche to saye
> as O father father: & this thy sonne taught vs
> by whome (as minister) thou givest us all thynge:
> That whan we were as it were borne again by thy spyrite
> and at the font stone in baptyme
> renounced and forsaken our father the devill
> and had begon to have no father in erthe
> than we shulde aknowledge onely oure father celestyall:
> By whose marveylous power we were made somewhat of ryght nought:
> by whose goodnesse we were restored
> whan we were loste: by whose wysedome incomparable
> evermore we are governed & kepte
> that we fall nat agayne in to distruction.[18]

While the actual content of the *Devout Treatise* is of course Erasmus's work, and Margaret has translated it faithfully, it is longer than the original and there are some parts that Margaret's use of language is more descriptive, or she uses different, more emphasising words to try to labour a point. There could also have been an element of her wanting to 'show off' her abilities in doing this, or perhaps this was an attempt to anglicise the language and therefore make the actual text more accessible to an English audience.[19] She uses doublet translations for Latin words, such as 'verity and truth' where Erasmus had simply written a singular word, '*veritas*'. And she uses a conversational style, similar to her father's way of writing used in *Utopia*, where she uses less formal styles of language and tries to draw the reader in, as if the piece was written just for them.

While we may never know her personal reasons for going ahead with such a controversial publication, and despite it being a difficult process to actually publish her work, with the help of Richard Hyrde and others Margaret managed to bring out her *Devout Treatise upon the Paternoster,* in English. The publishers were linked to the Mores through a family member, John Rastell, Sir Thomas's brother-in-law and Margaret's uncle. He, along with Thomas Berthelet, a Frenchman living in London and skilled printer, were able to arrange the printing and distribute the work on Margaret's behalf. Berthelet in particular was well connected, and in 1530 he would become Henry VIII's personal printer and bookbinder. Both men were members of her father's humanist group, and through this connection the work done by Erasmus and others, including Margaret, was able to be published on the continent, mainly in the Low Countries, distributed widely and come to be in the hands of humanists and reformists all over England.[20]

Even amongst the reformist community, there were mixed feelings about both Erasmus and Margaret's involvement. In Margaret's case, her education had caused stirs, and now she had entered the argument directly by showing women could indeed complete work of a very high standard, and that they were an active part in the humanist movement and reformist cause. It may well have been in an effort to quash any negativity that was felt about Margaret's work, that Richard Hyrde wrote such a thorough and lengthy introduction. It was laid out as a letter or correspondence to 'the most studious and virtuous young maid, Frances S'. This is believed to be Frances Staverton, a cousin of Margarets, the daughter of Thomas More's sister, Joan, and another who may have spent some time in the More School.[21]

In his introduction Hyrde goes out of his way to emphasise the good intentions of the work, the piety with which it was completed, and the pious character of the person who translated it. Here is an extract where Hyrde describes Margaret, and in doing so is trying to persuade Frances (and the audience as a whole) that following the example of the author would be a very good thing indeed:

> For I neuer herde tell nor reed of any woman well lerned that ever was (as plentuous as well tonges be) spotted or infamed as vicious. But on the otherside many by their lernyng taken suche increase of goodnesse that many may beare them wytnesse of their vertue of whiche sorte I coulde reherse a great nombre bothe of olde tyme and late savynge that I wyll be contente as for nowe with one example of oure owne countre and tyme that is: this gentylwoman whiche translated this lytell boke herafter folowyng: whose vertuous cōversacion lyvyng and sadde demeanoure maye be profe evydente ynough what good lernynge dothe where it is surely roted: of whom other women may take example of prudēt humble and wyfely behavour, charitable & very christēn vertue with whiche she hath with goddes helpe endevoured her selfe no lesse to garnisshe her soule than it hath lyked his goodnesse

> with lovely beauty and comelynesse to garnysshe and sette out her body: And undouted is it that to thyncrease of her vertue she hath taken and taketh no lytell occasyon of her lernyng besydes her other manyfolde and great cōmodyteis taken of the same amonge whiche cōmodyteis this is nat the leest that with her vertuous worshipfull wyse and well lerned husbande she hath by the occasyon of her lernynge and his delyte therin suche especiall conforte pleasure and pastyme as were nat well possyble for one unlerned couple eyther to take togyther or to concevue in their myndes what pleasure is therin.[22]

While this is just a small extract of his introduction, throughout the whole piece he goes to great pains to argue for the education of a woman, and to encourage other women to read the work and to follow the example of *'this gentylwoman whiche translated this lytell boke herafter folowyng'*. In drawing attention to Margaret's *'prudēnt humble and wyfely behavour, charitable & very christēn vertue'*, Hyrde is attempting to show that this type of academic work does not put the woman's virtues at risk, as had been argued by detractors of women's learning. He also draws on examples from antiquity, and shows that women have long been capable and should therefore be allowed to continue. In fact, his argument appears to show that it is an ideal that both husband and wife be equally well educated, so that they are able to have a happy marriage. This echoes the things we have already explored about Thomas More and his attitude towards education for both Joanna and Alice.

The use of the descriptor 'lytell' or little is also interesting. While to our modern eyes and ears it may come across as condescending, it may have been another tactic of Hyrde's, to shrink down the size of the work, and therefore it's inherent threat to those who were critical; after all, it's only one 'little book'.

Hyrde's involvement may also have allowed for more mainstream acceptance of the work of a woman. His reputation, while not necessarily huge, very much showed the reader that there was some gravitas, from the school of Thomas More, and from the court in general. But, despite this, the work was still controversial and in 1526 Thomas Berthelet found himself threatened with prosecution by the Bishop of London's vicar-general, Dr Richard Foxford.[23] In October 1524, just a few days after the date of the first printing of Margaret's translation, all printers and booksellers had been told to apply for licences for all religious texts, including translations. When he came to reprint the work in 1526, however, Berthelet had failed to apply for one, and had, therefore, to appear in court over the printing of 'a certain work called *The Treatise of the Paternoster* translated by the wife of Master Roper'. He was required to attend the consistory court on the 4 May 1526. However, before that date could arrive, Richard Hyrde had asked his friend Stephen Gardiner, recently appointed Wolsey's secretary, to intercede on Margaret's (and his own) behalf. After Gardiner spoke to Wolsey, and given Wolsey's position and fondness for More, and the humanist cause, Berthelet was allowed to reprint the work immediately and was not expected to attend court on this matter. As a result of this intercession by Wolsey, in this reprint we find the work's title pages are covered in artwork designed to appease the highest people in the land; there is the crest of Thomas Wolsey, hastily drawn, with mistakes but still recognisable as a homage, as well as the cap and cross of the cardinal or papal legate, and then surrounding this in the borders are the Tudor rose and the pomegranate, associated with King Henry and Queen Catherine respectively.[24] Appealing to Queen Catherine would have been something that Hyrde especially would have known to do; when Juan Luis Vives published his *De Institutione* he had dedicated it to Queen Catherine, therefore her attachment to the cause of women's education was something they hoped would allow the work to be accepted, and even perhaps adopted by a wider audience.

This was a close call for Margaret; thanks to her connections and those of her friends, she was able to avoid any direct involvement with legalities to do with her work. However, had there not been those willing to take on her cause, friendly humanists who were able to avert legal action and possible heresy charges, albeit for some selfish reasons, this could have been the end of the road for Margaret and possibly for the whole More family through association. As it played out Margaret was able to continue on and as these events took place when she was still a young mother that must have been a great relief to her as well as her husband and family.

Chapter 5

Motherhood

1523

While her father was busy climbing the political career ladder, and Margaret was busy translating the works of Erasmus, she and her husband were beginning to set up their own future. They both lived most of the time at Chelsea, for convenience for William's work as well as to continue to be part of the More household and school. They were close also to William's family who lived in Eltham, Kent, just a short journey out of the city. The couple had a small home in Eltham, close to the Ropers estate but it is unclear how much time they spent there. The Ropers also had a home in the parish of St Dunstan's church in Canterbury, and it is here that we have more evidence that they spent time here throughout their marriage.

However, it was at Chelsea that they made their home base, and especially in 1523, when Margaret fell pregnant with their first child, the family home and support became even more important to them both. Pregnancy was a challenging time for early modern women, who faced the prospect of complications and actually giving birth without the help of any sorts of modern medicine. There was no reliable test to prove that a woman was indeed pregnant, and while, just like today, there were signs, symptoms and general theories that would help to identify a possible pregnancy, many women did not know for certain until they felt the baby move for the first time. Most women start to feel movement from around four months onwards, but in some rare cases no movement is felt until even later than this. Once a pregnancy was identified, a woman was expected to maintain her normal routine, while ensuring they remain calm and do not put themselves under any stress or strain. Medicine at the time was dictated by the 'humours' within the body of blood, yellow bile, black bile and phlegm. If a woman complained of morning sickness, she may be told to limit her intake of fish or milk which were both considered phlegmatic, both of which modern doctors would recommend she eat.[1]

Once it was considered that the baby was due to arrive a woman would enter confinement. This was a period when the mother-to-be would be isolated within her room or rooms, attended to only by her close companions and, in some cases, midwife. The windows would be shuttered, usually curtains would be hung, and the fires in the room would be kept lit to keep the room warm, regardless of the time of year. The air-flow in the room would be stifled and lighting kept to a minimum to make the room as calm as possible. All this was done as the common thought at the time was that illness was carried on the air, and by restricting air coming into the room by closing windows and limiting who could enter, the mother and baby would be protected from disease. A woman would enter this period anything up to a few weeks before the baby was thought to be due. As there was little way of knowing when the baby was precisely due, this wasn't always an exact science. Royal and noble ladies often entered confinement upwards of a month prior to when physicians and midwives thought the baby would arrive, in an effort to stop any mishaps occurring with the mother or the child. In less affluent households, women would only enter something resembling confinement when the baby showed signs of imminent arrival, at which point midwives and relatives would be summoned.

Margaret entered confinement in the late stages of her pregnancy in late 1523. She was surrounded by her stepmother Alice, and her sisters and companions. At just 18 years of age, Margaret had been married for almost two years when she gave birth to a daughter, Elizabeth. We do not know how the birth went, or how Margaret felt being a first-time mother with all the risk this entailed. Some studies have shown that statistically, up to one in three women of childbearing age would succumb to some sort of problem relating to childbirth or pregnancy.[2] Another statistic puts the rate of death in childbirth at up to 18 per 1,000, compared to more modern statistics which show a rate of less than 3 per 1,000. The risks that came with carrying a baby and giving birth were all too clear to all early modern women and everyone at this time would have known, either directly or by word of mouth, of someone who had developed complications and had died.[3] Women who were experienced at giving birth would often take a lead role in helping mothers to overcome their fears and, through their experience, hopefully avoid these types of complications. However, the number of women who died during or after childbirth meant that is was still an undertaking and would often mean that priests would bless the mother prior to entering confinement, and even the vehemently religious would fall back on old-wives tales and talismans for good luck or to tell their fortunes.[4]

Margaret would probably have been attended by a midwife, who was a woman of 'good standing' as described by Alison Sim, who would have the expertise of having attended numerous births in the local area. Families would often employ the same midwife to attend all their births, and it was not uncommon for generations of women to be served by the same midwife. She would be responsible for the health of the mother during the birth, and ensuring that everything ran smoothly, and when the baby eventually arrived, she would be the one to wrap it and present it to the father.[5] If a baby was born sickly, she would also be the most likely to perform a baptism rite, to ensure that the baby's soul would be able to enter heaven. We do not have a record of who was midwife to Margaret at any of her births, but given that her stepsister, Alice, had already had children by this point also, it would probably have been someone well known to the family.

Not long after the birth, a newborn Elizabeth would have been taken by her father and the wider family to be baptised. In 1523, it is unclear whether the family were still at The Barge in Bucklersbury or had made the move across to Chelsea, so Elizabeth may well have been baptised in the same church as her mother, St Stephen's. The baptism itself would have been a time for the family to celebrate the safe arrival of the child, and also to formally name her.

Children were normally named for relatives or after important or influential people. Margaret's sister Elizabeth was most likely in turn named for Thomas More's sister, Elizabeth, who was married to John Rastell, the publisher and fellow humanist who helped Margaret to publish her work. The name Elizabeth is therefore one that meant a great deal to the More family, as well as being popular and fashionable at the time more generally.

The baptism ceremony would have looked very similar to the one we are familiar with today, with prayers said for the child's future, the child being welcomed into God's family and promises made by godparents to take responsibility for the child's spiritual wellbeing. We do not know who Margaret and William chose as godparents, records of that nature were not kept at this time, but given how close the whole family were, it is likely that Margaret's sisters and members of the extended family would have been given these roles for all the families' children.

Margaret would not have been present at the baptism, though as following birth a woman would be required to keep her confinement for a further period of forty days, after which she would need to be 'churched'. Churching is a ceremonial act of welcoming back, thanksgiving and of cleansing following the act of childbirth. Margaret would have attended church after her confinement had finished, dressed in her best clothes, where the priest would have anointed her once again with holy water and blessed her. A similar prayer is offered up today, and may well have been what Margaret would have heard at her own churching ceremonies:

> Almighty, everlasting God, through the delivery of the blessed Virgin Mary, Thou hast turned into joy the pains of the faithful in childbirth; look mercifully upon this Thy handmaid, coming in gladness to Thy temple to offer up her thanks: and grant that after this life, by the merits and intercession of the same blessed Mary, she may merit to

arrive, together with her offspring, at the joys of everlasting happiness. Through Christ our Lord.⁶

Following the churching, Margaret would have returned to the family home and been able to carry on life as normal, with her new baby, husband and the rest of her family.

Elizabeth was the first of five children that Margaret and William had together. Four of them within ten years; Elizabeth in 1523, then Margaret arrived in 1526, Mary around 1529 and then a boy, Thomas, in 1533. This was almost a mirror image of her own sibling group, three sisters and then a brother. Margaret was named for her mother, and Mary was likely a reflection of the Virgin Mary and in reverence to Princess Mary. Thomas was named for his grandfather, in a similar way to how Margaret's brother John had been named for his grandfather, Sir John More. Their fifth child, a boy named Anthony, would arrive much later in 1544 when Margaret was around 39 years old, and Elizabeth, their eldest child was 21. His name appears to be different to the rest of his siblings, with some speculating that his name came from Sir Thomas More's work *A Dialogue of Comfort against Tribulation*, written in the Tower during his incarceration, one of the main characters in this piece was called Anthony. Another theory is that he is named after St Anthony of Padua, the patron saint of lost things; as an unexpected baby it may have occurred to Margaret and William to name their child for a saint as a 'blessing'.⁷

The arrival of grandchildren, especially the children of Margaret, must have been a source of great happiness to Sir Thomas, who we have already seen, enjoyed having children in his home. While Margaret was still pregnant with Elizabeth, he wrote to her to congratulate her on her pregnancy and to wish her well with the impending birth:

> In your letter you speak of your approaching confinement. We pray most earnestly that all may go happily and successfully with you. May God and our Blessed Lady grant you happily and safely a little one like to his mother in everything except sex. Yet let it by all means be a girl, if only she will make up for the inferiority of her sex by her zeal to imitate her mother's virtue and learning. Such a girl I would prefer to three boys. Goodbye, my dearest child.[8]

Even Erasmus got in on the act of congratulating the new parents. He dedicated his 1523 publication of his *Commentary of the Christmas Hymn of Prudentias* to Margaret, and when he wrote to her to tell her about this, he wrote:

> William Roper ... has given you (or if you prefer it, you have given him) the most fortunate first-fruits of your union, or to put it better, each has given the other a child – to whom a kiss is to be sent.[9]

While Erasmus may not have ever met the children, or visited, his affection for Margaret and the whole More family is shown clearly in this letter, which he ends by saying, 'A warm farewell to you who are not a lesser light of the age and Britain. Greet also for me the whole of your choir (school).'

As had been the case for Margaret when she was growing up, the women of the household would have been responsible for the raising of all the children, with Lady Alice More, who was known as Dame Alice following her husband's knighthood, taking the lead as mistress of the household. Margaret would not necessarily have been expected to have been a hands-on mother, but there are no records suggesting the employment of a wetnurse, and with the closeness of the family in the house at Chelsea it is likely that in fact Margaret, with the help of her siblings, husband and others, took an active role in her children's upbringing. The time between the births of her children also suggests that, unlike in the case of her own mother, Margaret was not pregnant straight away after each birth, and therefore may well have been feeding the babies herself. It is also likely that given the marriages of her sisters in 1525 (Elizabeth and Cecily) and of Margaret Giggs in 1526 that the household was very much set up for mothers and babies, with lots of help for the many children that the More sisters went on to have. Alice, her stepsister had seven children in total; three with her first husband and then a further four with Giles Alington. Margaret Giggs and John Clement had seven children also, as did Elizabeth and William Dauncey. Cecily and Giles Heron had at least three. The More household would appear to have been a particularly fecund family and this must have pleased Thomas, the doting grandfather.

Margaret's other responsibility after dealing with her children was to run the 'household' of her husband, William Roper. While she had lived at home with her father and stepmother she would have learned the mechanics of this job from Alice; housekeeping, managing any servants, meals and the household accounts were all the responsibility of the wife, the mistress of the house. Margaret, in the capacity of Mistress Roper, would have had responsibility for the family unit and their own belongings, servants, houses and lands that they owned or leased. The homes they were given by the Roper family on their marriage would have fallen under this remit, and while William would probably not have left his wife to deal with everything, especially while pregnant or dealing with very young children, she would have been very involved in decisions.

Alongside these two homes in Kent, at some point following the move to Chelsea, probably after the birth of Elizabeth, the Ropers started to use 'Butts Close', the small self-contained building in the grounds of Chelsea, as their home also. While it is easy to imagine that Sir Thomas was not happy to give up his retreat, it may have been necessary given how many people were now living, either partly or full-time, in their home at Chelsea. It may well have been that, given their circumstances, moving the Ropers out of Chelsea into their own dwelling freed up more of the Chelsea home and also allowed Margaret and William more privacy and time with their young family.

One aspect of parenting that we know that Margaret paid a great deal of attention to was her children's education. As we have already explored, the education of young children fell primarily to their mothers, but in Margaret's case, she took this responsibility very seriously. Margaret took her father's 'school' as an example and tried to give all her own children a similar education to what she herself received. The girls, as well as Thomas, all received a classical education and learned Latin, Greek and classics, just as Margaret and her siblings had done before them. The Ropers hired tutors also, most notable of whom were John Christopherson, who would go on to be Chaplain to Queen Mary I, and John Morwen. Both of these men were known for their work in classics and worked themselves and translated work to and from Greek.[10] Translation would form a major part of the children's education as it had done for Margaret, and this would have a massive influence in particular on her daughter, Mary.

Mary showed that she had an aptitude for learning very similar to that of her mother, and this must have been welcomed and encouraged by both Margaret, and if this had been apparent in her early years, by Sir Thomas also. Mary was born in *c.*1529, and so would have been young indeed when the family were all living in Chelsea for prolonged periods, when Sir Thomas would have been very busy with matters of state while he was working as chancellor to Henry VIII. While Thomas may have had an influence on the children's upbringing, and Margaret's high standards for their education, their early and formative years saw their grandfather very much taken away from them for long spans of time, and his influence on them would probably have been more indirect, through his letters and writings in later years, and through his faith.

Faith was something that the More family had always taken seriously, and as a mother, Margaret would continue this tradition. The whole family would still partake in Bible passages at mealtimes, pray together every day, and attend the local parish church, Chelsea Old Church. Even when Sir Thomas was at the height of his powers, he would still attend the local church, which caused some issues amongst the nobility at court, believing this to be unbecoming of his station. William Roper recounts a story

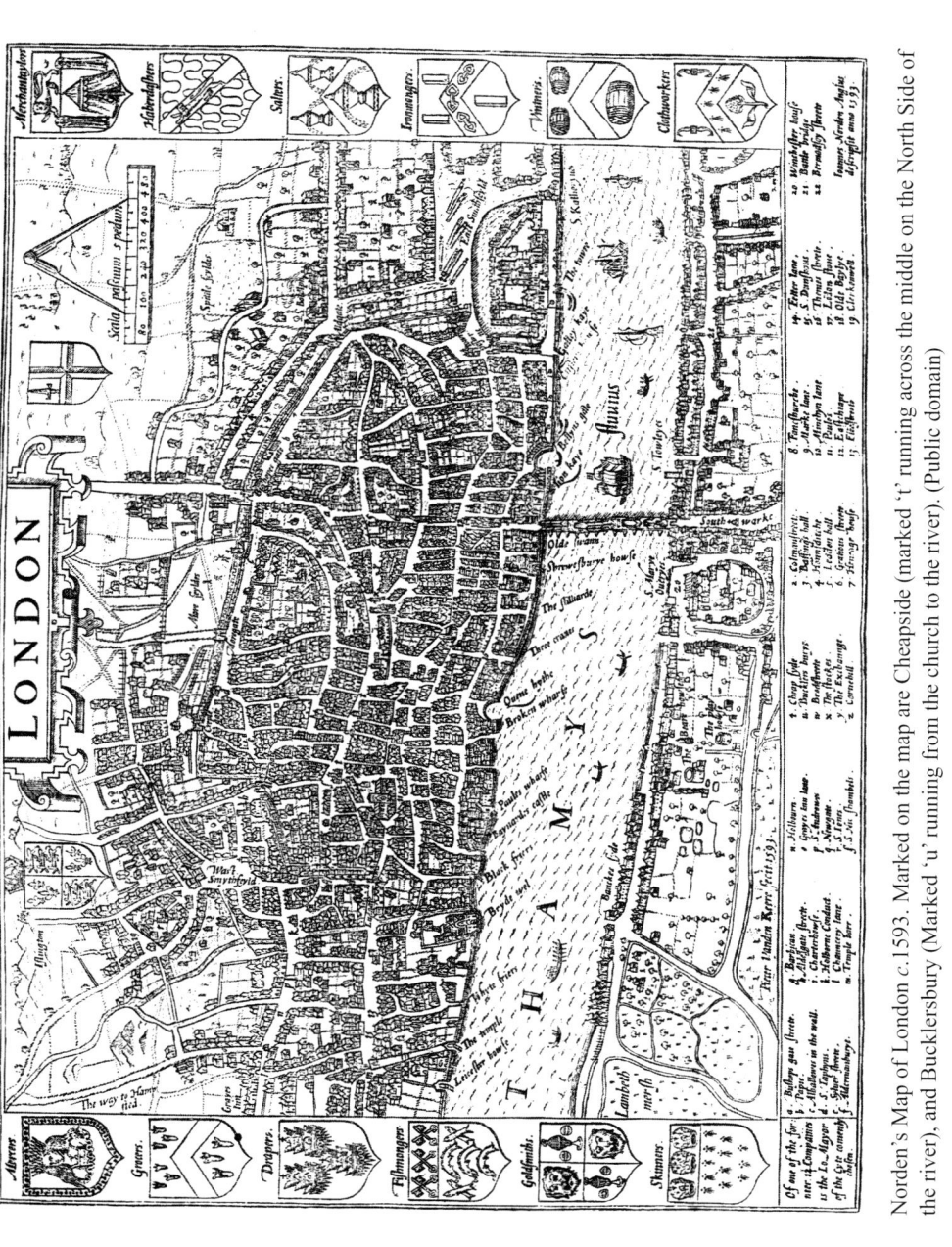

Norden's Map of London c.1593. Marked on the map are Cheapside (marked 't' running across the middle on the North Side of the river), and Bucklersbury (Marked 'u' running from the church to the river). (Public domain)

Portrait of Desiderius Erasmus of Rotterdam by Hans Holbein the Younger c. 1532. (Public domain)

Front cover image of Margaret More Roper's translation of Erasmus – A Devout Treatise upon the Paternoster (1524). (Public domain)

The More family portrait by Hans Holbein the Younger c.1530. (Public domain)

Portraits of Margaret More Roper and William Roper by Hans Holbein the Younger *c*.1535. (Public domain)

The Roper Gate in Canterbury. (Author's own)

Exterior of the Roper Chapel at St Dunstan's Church, Canterbury. (Author's own, with permission from St Dunstan's Church)

Interior of the Roper Chapel, with incomplete tombs. (Author's own, with permission from St Dunstan's Church)

A modern stained glass from St Dunstan's Church, Canterbury depicting St Thomas More, his wife Alice, Margaret More and William Roper. (Author's own)

'Sir Thomas More and his Daughter', by John Rogers Herbert (1844). (Public domain)

'Margaret Roper Rescuing the Head of her Father', by Lucy Madox Browne (1873).

of the Duke of Norfolk happening upon Sir Thomas singing in the choir at the church, and he admonished him:

God body! God body! My Lord Chancellor, a parish clerk! You dishonour the King and his office.

'Nay', quoth Sir Thomas More, smiling upon the Duke, 'your grace may not think that the King, your master and mine, will with me, for serving of God, his master, be offended, or thereby count his office dishonoured.'[11]

The family were all, for the most part, devoted followers of the traditional church teachings. They all spoke out against the reformist, Protestant teachings that were becoming popular, and in 1523 Sir Thomas wrote his *Response to Luther*, in which he spoke up against the reforms suggested by Martin Luther and his new beliefs, and his criticism of the Roman Catholic Church. This was following Henry VIII himself writing his defence of the pope and the Catholic Church, for which he was awarded the title of *Fidei Defensor*, Defender of the Faith, a title that is still used by English monarchs to the present day.

Thomas's *Defence* was one of the events which singled him out in the eyes of Henry VIII and saw him quickly elevated to a knighthood and then to the chancellorship, as the king felt that Thomas's and his own thoughts matched so perfectly. Indeed, the whole family were in good graces with King Henry, who in November 1525, invited them all, including Margaret and her sisters, to court.[12] The reason for the visit was for the king to be able to see, in person, what the More School and the subjects it taught looked like in reality. His illegitimate son, Henry Fitzroy, was just starting his school years and Henry wanted to know what would be best for him to learn. Even for boys, too much learning was viewed as a bad idea and would make them cowardly. But Henry himself had received a scholarly education and he knew of the reputation of Sir Thomas's family, and so he wanted to discuss their educational experiences with them in person. They prepared well for the meeting at which all the More daughters were asked to make an argument for the Quintillian problem, one they were very familiar with. They obviously made a good impression, as Henry Fitzroy's tutor said in a letter to Sir Thomas after the event: 'When your daughters disputed in philosophy afore the King's grace I would it had been my fortune to be present.'[13]

The family would have been dressed up in their finest to meet the king, and for Margaret and her sisters to be able to perform before the king and to show the extent of their learning, wit and intelligence, must have been very exciting for them all. According to later accounts, Margaret's own argument won the day and impressed everyone present.

The family's loyalty to their faith was, therefore, something that not only they were proud of, but something that was making their lives better through Sir Thomas's friendship and shared beliefs with the king. It must have been a severe shock for all the More family when, in 1525, William Roper converted to the Lutheran, reformist faith. He purchased books, including one of the earliest copies of Tyndale's Bible to have entered England, he attended events and spoke out in favour of the reforms at family gatherings. He, according to Guy, rejected the recommended reading of his wife and father-in-law and instead chose materials that were suspected of being heretical. One such book, *Image of Love*, was recalled by Bishop Tunstall, and Sir Thomas was tasked by Cardinal Wolsey with rounding up copies and also any merchants who may have or plan to sell copies in future.

Following a raid of a merchants at a precinct called Steelyards, around Christmas 1525, the men who were arrested gave William Roper's name as a buyer of the book and this meant that he would face the same charge of heresy and possession of heretical materials as they did. Luckily for William, his father-in-law's position and Wolsey's generosity once again saved the family from facing charges of heresy. Margaret was pregnant with their second child at the time and, out of desperation, asked for her father to intercede on her behalf and try to bring William back to the true faith, to save his soul, and probably to try to avoid any further threats to their lives.

In response to this request, Sir Thomas is supposed to have said:

> Meg, I have borne a long time with thy husband; I have reasoned and argued with him in these points of religion, and still given to him my poor fatherly counsel, but I perceive none of all this able to call him home; and therefore, Meg, I will no longer dispute with him, but will clean give him over and get me to God and pray for him.[14]

According to another source, 'Sir Thomas during that time [was the man] whom then of all the world [William Roper] did most abhor.'[15]

William and Sir Thomas's relationship had broken down completely. Sir Thomas had effectively given William over to God, and to prayers to change his mind, and William for his part was unhappy with the treatment he was receiving from his father-in-law. This put pressure on Margaret; trapped between her husband and her beloved father, she could only hope and pray that there would be a reconciliation and that her husband would find his way back to her side. William did in fact convert back to Catholicism and he would remain so until he died. For the remainder of their marriage, William and Margaret were both devout Catholics and this continued through to their children and later generations of the family.

After the events of 1525 and 1526 had mercifully blown over, Margaret's and William's lives appear to settle down somewhat. They added to their family, and appeared to enjoy splitting their times between their homes at Chelsea with the rest of the More family, and in Eltham and Canterbury with the Ropers. William, having passed the bar in early 1525, was working in various legal roles in the city, and from 1529 onwards would also serve as a member of parliament. Margaret devoted her life to her family, and to ensuring that her own children were given the best and most stable upbringing and education that she could provide for them. The piety of the More household and their continuous learning kept them together and Sir Thomas's love of having his family around him meant that Chelsea was a hub for all things, both religious and in terms of the family members' careers.

It seemed like a quiet life for the family, and Thomas's career kept going from strength to strength. He was being trusted with more and more responsibility, and had the ear and support of

Henry VIII. When, in 1528, Cardinal Wolsey's position at court began to be undermined, it was to Sir Thomas that the king turned to try to stabilise the court and to solve the problems that the cardinal had been unable to find a solution for. Thomas would take on the role of chancellor with vigour, and his humanist beliefs led him to attempt to utilise his position to act against the Protestant reforms that had almost claimed his own son-in-law.

Chapter 6

Humanism and Reputation

1526

Margaret's own love of learning and her devotion to her faith continued throughout her adult life and, even when busy with responsibilities for her own children, she was still very much a studious and curious individual. The family would partake in prayers and acts of worship throughout the day and, if Sir Thomas was away on business or unable to lead, Margaret was a key person in ensuring that everyone in the household maintained their routine correctly. William Roper describes a typical day for the family as:

> Sir Thomas More's custom was daily, if he were at home, besides his private prayers, with his children to say seven psalms, litany and suffrages following, so was his guise nightly, before he went to bed, with his wife, children and household to go to his chapel and there upon his knees ordinarily to say certain psalms and collects with them.[1]

From this description, we can gather an impression of just how important the prayers and worship were to the family and to their daily routines. All the family members also had work, particularly charitable endeavours that they each took responsibilities for, as well as helping each other as much as possible. Each would have taken turns in reading at family prayer times, and all would have had personal copies of books of hours and common prayers which would allow them to pray privately and explore their own faith.

Another act of piety that Sir Thomas is known for is that he commonly wore a hair shirt. Wearing a hair shirt was something usually done by monks or priests, as a way of doing penance, or causing discomfort as a way of atoning for sins. The wearing of a hair shirt, or a *cilice,* was even then seen as somewhat archaic and was not something commonly done by lay-people. Sir Thomas is said to have taken to wearing one daily; very few people were aware of him doing so, with one of those few being Margaret.

The matter of him wearing the hair shirt came to light one evening when Anne Cresacre spotted the garment poking out from beneath his clothes. According to Roper, it was a warm summer's evening and, as he took off his jacket to cool off, the hair shirt poked out from the top of his shirt, where there was no collar covering his neck.[2] Anne was amused by this, as it was a very unusual thing to see. Roper writes: 'My wife, not ignorant of his manner perceiving the same, privily told him of it and her, being sorry that she saw it, presently amended it.'

The fact that Sir Thomas trusted his daughter with this knowledge of something so very personal is evidence of the close bond that they shared. By contrast, early in their marriage his wife, Alice, had previously attempted to convince him to stop wearing it; perhaps this is why it was something that Margaret and Sir Thomas shared, and Alice chose to leave alone in later years.

The reputation that Sir Thomas and the family gained through shared experience of these activities, meant that Margaret was starting to build a name for herself, particularly in humanist circles. This reputation stretched far and wide, even as far as the Mediterranean, Spain and North Africa. In a copy of the Qu'ran, now located in the Bodleian Library in Oxford, historians have found a coded message which reads:

and for because I would
not but that I should
be in remembrance of
people and not forgot
ten the marvelous gret
existence of one so noble so wise so
coning of verte
us as he whose name is
callid Thomas More
knight lord chancellor
of England the
to and twenty yere
of king henry the
eight and he had
thre daughters exel
ently lernid in the
laten Greec and Hebrew
whose names were Margaret
Bes and Cecile of whom in
special Margret Roper was
alone the most noble of

any that ever lived in
this world for beauty for
scince for virtue for ex-
elence as she wose servant
I have ever bene.³

This note is particularly interesting due to a number of different factors. It is located in a copy of the Qu'ran that originated from Spain. Spain had a large Muslim population due to its occupation of Moorish Northern Africa, and even though the Moors had officially been expelled, their influence carried on into the sixteenth century in the culture, language and the religious diversity.

The year mentioned in the text, '*to and twenty yere*', is 1531, when the king and his wife, Queen Catherine of Aragon, who was Spanish, were in dispute and Henry VIII was trying to divorce her. In 1531, Sir Thomas was still chancellor, and he was struggling to give the king the divorce he wanted, and this was taken by some as support for the Spanish Queen Catherine. This may account for the fact that this message of support for Sir Thomas, his daughters, and, by extension, the queen, was in code. It may have been felt, even then, that to express allegiance in this way would have been controversial. There were links between the More family and Spain, particularly through Juan Luis Vives, who while staying with the Mores had become friends with not only Sir Thomas but also with Margaret and her sisters. It is possibly through these links that Margaret's reputation spread as far afield, and into Arabic and Islamic scholarship, within her own lifetime.⁴

Her reputation had been built on her intellectual abilities and through the distribution of her printed works. We only have one piece of work definitely and wholly attributed to her that has survived, but some accounts, including that of her husband and family members, speak of poetry, letters and other writings and translations that were familiar to them. While we will never know if there were other lost works that Margaret put her name to, it seems probable that she did produce other writings during her lifetime and given that she had been so determined to get her translation of Erasmus into print, it is likely that she tried to do the same for other pieces of her work. While the mixed reception, and the possible legal ramifications, may have put her off a little, she wrote letters to her father continuously and studied throughout her lifetime, and so it is likely that there was more of a foundation to her reputation, as a translator, writer, poet or humanist, than perhaps we are aware of today.

Margaret's own involvement in the humanist movement, albeit mostly through her father's connections and works, was still a tangible and real one. She worked with him in his office from time to time, discussing his work and offering opinions, was held in the highest esteem by those connected with her father, and mentioned in correspondence in her own right. We can see this through the concern that was shown when in 1527 she fell ill; it was the sweating sickness that coursed through the country at regular intervals. William Roper gives us a description of events:

> At such time as my wife, as many other that year were, was sick of the sweating sickness; who, lying in so great extremity of the disease as by no invention of devices that physicians in such cases commonly use (of whom she had divers both expert, wise and well-learned, then continuously attendant about her) she could be kept from sleep – so that both

physicians and all other there despaired of her recovery, and gave her over. Her father, as her that most entirely tendered her, being in no small heaviness for her, by prayer at God's hand sought to get her a remedy.

Whereupon going up, after his usual manner, into his aforesaid New Building, this in his chapel, upon his knees, with tears most devoutly besought Almighty God that it would like his goodness, unto whom nothing was impossible, if it were his blessed will, at his meditation to vouchsafe graciously to hear his humble petition. Where incontinent came into his mind that a Glister should be the only way to help her. Which, when he told the physicians, they by and by confessed that, if there were any hope of health, that was the very best help indeed, much marvelling at themselves that they had not before remembered it.

Then was it immediately ministered unto her sleeping, which she could by no means have been brought unto waking. And albeit after that she was thereby fully awakened, God's marks, an evident undoubted token of death, plainly appeared upon her; yet she, contrary to all expectation was, as it was thought, by her father's fervent prayer miraculously recovered, and at length again to perfect health restored.[5]

Upon hearing of her illness, Erasmus offered his condolences, and More himself wrote that, 'if it had pleased God at that time to have taken [her] to his mercy, he would never have meddled with worldly matters after.'[6]

The *glister* mentioned in the passage refers to an enema, not something that was routinely used to treat the sweating sickness according to most other sources, and appears to have been suggested entirely by Sir Thomas. He did have a good knowledge of medicine, so it is plausible that this may have been the case that he made this suggestion based on his own medical opinion. It appears from the tone of the writing, however, that Roper certainly believed that the answer came to Sir Thomas through prayer, and it was God's own intervention that spared his wife's life. Perhaps, coming so soon after his brush with Wolsey and the heresy laws for his Lutheran leanings, it was this 'miraculous' recovery that helped to convert him back to Catholicism.

Thankfully, Margaret made a full recovery, and life was able to return to normal. There was a great deal of excitement in the More house from 1527 onwards, as Sir Thomas was called away more, given tasks abroad and at court by Cardinal Wolsey and also by the king directly. He was also working hard to combat the heresies that were becoming more and more prevalent, and under the instruction of his friend Bishop Cuthbert Tunstall, he was given dispensation to read the books that were considered heretical in order for him to come up with some arguments against them. Tunstall persuaded him by telling him that he 'dearest brother, are as distinguished in the use of our native language as you are in Latin'. Tunstall was so impressed by what he saw, in the summer of 1529 he took Sir Thomas with him in the party which went to Cambrai, where they were to negotiate a peace treaty between England and the powers on the continent: King Francis I of France, and Emperor Charles V of the Holy Roman Empire.

Upon his return, a fire broke out at Chelsea while Sir Thomas was still with the king at Woodstock, and, according to Roper, the barns which contained that year's harvest of corn were burnt down, with damage also done to the main house. This must have been a distressing event for all concerned and the More family lost a number of buildings, as well as a substantial amount of income due to the damage. However, as Reynolds points out, the fire was the least of Sir Thomas's worries, as while he and Bishop Tunstall had been away at Cambrai, the legatine court at Blackfriars had been hearing the case for the king's divorce from Catherine of Aragon. When Sir Thomas returned, the case had not come down in the king's favour and this spelled the downfall of Wolsey. Within weeks, the cardinal was ousted from his role as chancellor and in late October 1529, Sir Thomas was presented with the Great Seal of Office.

Throughout all these events, Margaret and the rest of the More household had been attempting to carry on with life as normal; normal for the Mores meant accommodating visitors from various places and backgrounds. In late 1526, one such visitor came at the behest of Erasmus himself, when he asked Sir Thomas and his family to provide lodgings for a talented artist, to allow him, hopefully, to gain some work in London, and perhaps attract a mentor or two. That artist was Hans Holbein the Younger. In a letter to Peter Gilles, a Dutch acquaintance who he also introduced the artist to, he describes how Holbein would not find work in the Low Countries (Holland and Belgium) for 'here the arts are coldly treated, so he makes for England in the hope of collecting some golden angels'. The 'golden angels' in this quote refers to the English coin, the angel-noble, and shows the friendliness between the two men, as he is able to make this descriptive wordplay.

When Holbein arrived in England, he carried with him two letters of recommendation: one addressed to Archbishop Warham, the other to Sir Thomas More. Sir Thomas took the artist in and tried to help him to find work, writing: 'Your painter, my dearest Erasmus, is a wonderful artist; but I fear he will not find England the rich and fertile field he had hoped; however, lest he find it quite barren, I will do what I can.'[7]

To follow up this promise to *'do what I can'*, Thomas commissioned the young artist to paint a large and ambitious portrait of the entire More family. It would also appear that Erasmus' letter to William Warham worked, and he painted his portrait at this time too, producing a work for him in 1527. The portrait is a life-size rendition of the whole family, within their own home at Chelsea, and encompasses three generations including John More, Thomas's father, and all Thomas's children, adopted children and members of the extended household.[8] The original portrait is unfortunately lost, but we do have original sketches of the group and individuals that have been preserved, and two copies which were taken from the original have also survived for us to study.

In the portrait, we can see Margaret in great detail, pictured as she is in the very front of the group, and sitting in the centre of the women pictured. She is seated, hands resting on a book, holding the page so as not to lose her place. This is a theme that we find with all the Holbein portraits we have of Margaret, and even in later portraits, also painted from life at a later time and date: she is featured still with a book. This would be to symbolise her learning and her association with the printed word. Looking at the other women in the portrait, however, we can see that most of them are featured with a book, actively reading, except one resting on Cecily's lap. Even son, John More, is featured as a scholar. Elsewhere in the picture we see more books piled on tables behind the sitters, as well as musical instruments, and above their heads, a fine example of a mechanical clock; quite the rarity and worthy of showing off as part of the room in their new Chelsea home. We can see the family seated in a lavishly decorated room, with wood panelling, drapes and large windows, and we even get a glimpse into the rest of the house where, in the background of the picture, a figure sits at a desk studying. The picture is striking in both its size and scale, and also its detail, which came to be something of a trademark of Holbein's work.

Once he had been commissioned to complete the piece, Holbein took detailed drawings of the group and also the individuals who are featured in the portrait. While the original study of Margaret does not survive, we do have a number of the others including Sir Thomas and Margaret Giggs. Holbein took these studies back to his studios on the continent, and when he returned he visited Erasmus to show him the work he had done. Erasmus was so moved that he wrote personally to Margaret to express his delight at having seen the picture, and also to tell her just how close a likeness Holbein had captured:

Erasmus Rotterdamus to Margaret Roper, Greetings.

I cannot find words, Margaret Roper, ornament of Britain, to express the delight I felt when Holbein's picture showed me your whole family almost as faithfully as if I had been among you. I often wish that, before my last day, I may look even once more on that most dear company to which I owe a great part of whatever fortune or glory I possess, and to none could I be more willingly indebted. The gifted hand of the painter has given me no small portion of my wish. I recognise you all, but no one better that yourself. I seem to behold through all your beautiful household a spirit shining that is still more beautiful. I congratulate you all in that family happiness, and most of all your excellent father ... I am writing this in the midst of overwhelming work and in poor health, therefore I must leave it to your skill to convince all your sisters that this is a fair letter and is written to each one of them no less than to yourself. Convey my respectful and affectionate salutations to the honoured Lady Alice, your mother; since I cannot kiss her, I kiss her picture. To my godson John More, I wish every happiness, and you will give a special greeting on my part to your most worthy husband Roper, so rightly dear to you.[9]

This letter is special as it not only conveys a sense that the likenesses in the painting were good, although as Erasmus had not visited the Mores much, his close friendship with Thomas must have meant that he was able to judge, at the very least, Holbein's depiction of his friend. The affection that Erasmus held for the whole family is made clear, and his respectful, if not entirely warm, greeting to Alice shows the respect that he had for her.

Margaret responded in kind, and this letter to her learned friend is the only surviving example of correspondence written in her own hand. The letter itself was probably written in late

1529, following her receipt of this letter above and the flow of the letter seems to show that she was using his letter to her as a reference point for her reply. This is one of very few occasions where we are able to hear Margaret's voice and see her written words, and for that reason this letter is a remarkable window into her life. She writes, as Erasmus had done to her, in Latin, but the translated letter reads:

Margaret Roper to the Most Learned Theologian D. Erasmus Rotterdamus, Greetings.

How a good thing can become most welcome when one enjoys it suddenly and unexpectedly, I recently, O most learned of men, found by experience to be quite true when your letter, no less elegant than affectionate, and a sure witness to your devotion to my father and all his family, was brought to me by your Talesius. As it came unexpectedly, so it brought the greater pleasure to my mind. For I have never dared to hope or expect that you, so fully occupied with so much important work, miserably and continually distressed be grievous sickness and worn out by the burden of age, that you should ever deem me worthy of the honour to which I have been raised by the favour of your letter. As often as I show it to anyone, I realise that from it no small praise will accrue to my reputation, which cannot be made more notable in any other way than by your letter. For what can be compared with the honour of which I am counted worthy, whom the glory of the whole world have honoured with this letter? Wherefore as your kindness has bestowed on me something far beyond my humble desert, so I indeed rightly acknowledge myself quote unequal to giving the thanks due to such a signal favour.

We freely acknowledge with the greatest gratitude that the arrival of the painter [Holbein] gave you so much pleasure because he brought you the portraits of both my parents and all of us. We pray for nothing more ardently than that we may some time be able to speak face to face with and see our teacher, by whose learned labours we have received whatever of good letters we have imbibed, and one who is the old and faithful friend of our father. Farewell.

My mother greets you heartily, and so do my husband who is entirely yours, and my brother. Both my sisters send you hearty greetings.[10]

This letter shows us many things, and while it is only a small sample of her writing, we can perhaps extract some clues about Margaret's personality and opinions. She spends a lot of time writing about the honour that he does her by writing to her, and by giving compliments to her as an individual. She is respectful, gushing, and verging on over-the-top with her gratitude at times, but this is tempered by the not-so-positive phrases referring to Erasmus's 'grievous sickness' and 'burden of age'. Perhaps this is a tongue-in-cheek reference to his well-known hypochondria, and a little bit of cheekiness from Margaret to temper what would at first glance appear to be an avalanche of compliments.

From when this letter was written in late 1529, the course of the More family life took a very different turn. Sir Thomas's role as chancellor meant that he was away from home even more, travelling with the king, and spending more time at court dealing with his responsibilities and tending to the king's wishes. His main focus fell into two issues: heresy, and the king's 'Great Matter'.

For Sir Thomas, heresy was the key priority. Despite his and the rest of the humanists working hard to bolster the position of the true faith and to eradicate heresies in England and beyond, the reformist movement was gaining in popularity. The movement and its followers, started in part by Martin Luther and then continued by other religious reformists such as John Calvin and Ulrich Zwingli, became known as 'Protestants'. All across Europe, Protestant groups sprang up and sought to challenge the Roman Catholic Church, accusing it of corruption and of keeping the teachings of the church from the people it was supposed to serve. In France and the Low Countries particularly, the movement gathered in pace and its followers were persecuted, executed, and burned at the stake as heretics. This led to further condemnation of the Catholic authorities and only served to fan the flames of the movement into something much larger. By 1530, the church had split even further and irrevocably, and calls for reformation came from all corners. It was a turbulent time and all across Europe there was a febrile religious atmosphere where reform and religious freedom and fervour were brewing at all levels of society.

The humanist community to which the Mores belonged started to fracture, some following the new learning into what they believed to be humanism's logical next step, others staying true to the old faith and maintaining the position that reform rather than wholesale change was what was required. The 'Protestant' reforms were a main talking point at dinner tables all across England too; book printers and sellers were producing more and more copies of Tyndale's Bible and other literature that was circulated amongst the literate, especially in the cities, with London being the hub of all their activities, and at the English court, the noble families formed factions around the reformist and more conservative, Catholic causes.

In response to this, Thomas decided to take action in the best way that he knew how: he picked up a pen. In 1529, he published *A Dialogue Concerning Heresies* which set out to outline his thoughts and policies on the new reformist movement and why it should not be allowed to propagate amongst the Christians of Europe. It was intended also to give Catholics the knowledge to be able to counter any heretical argument that they may be faced with:

A dialogue of Sir Thomas
More, Knight, one of the
Council of our sovereign lord the King, and Chancellor of his duchy of Lancaster. Wherein be
treated divers matters: as of the veneration and worship of images and relics,
praying to saints, and going on pilgrimage. With many other things touching the pestilent sect of Luther
and Tyndale, by the
one begun in
Saxony, and
by the
other labored

to be brought into England.
Newly overseen by the said Sir Thomas More,
Chancellor of England.
1530.[11]

This book was just one part of the arguments that were taking place within publications, and with Tyndale and others, such as Simon Fish, weighing in and producing works against the teachings and way of the Catholic Church, Thomas felt it his duty to try to bolster its position and perhaps, stop any more people following the ways of the 'new men'.

However, the writing was not enough, and More, in his position within the court and following orders firstly from Cardinal Wolsey and then carrying out his own policies, had to impose tough new policies when dealing with 'heretykes'. It started with the banning of books, and booksellers being punished for defying them, then he started to punish people with physical beatings and imprisonment, forcing them to deny their heretical ways. Such was the case of Thomas Bilney, who in 1526 was brought to trial for preaching heresy in London. The Cambridge scholar 'bore the faggot' and was imprisoned for eleven months for his crimes.[12] But things escalated at a pace while Sir Thomas was chancellor and six people were burned at the stake for heresy, with numerous others beaten, potentially tortured, put in the stocks, imprisoned and suffering other punishments. There is a great deal of scholarly debate about whether Sir Thomas was actually personally responsible for these burnings, punishments and torture, or whether his policies were simply taken to their natural end in a case of the end justifying the means for his loyal servants.

Foxe's Book of Martyrs appears to paint a picture of Sir Thomas having a great 'relish for burning heretics', but this is not something that we have much evidence for. In his biography of Sir Thomas, Peter Ackroyd uses Foxe's book to tell a story of how he 'tied heretics to a tree in his Chelsea garden and whipped them'.[13] Sir Thomas himself, in his *Apology* of 1533, denied ever having personal involvement with those who were burned, punished or tortured during the time he was responsible for such cases, claiming that he only ever personally punished two heretics. One was a child whom he caned in front of his family for heresy regarding the Eucharist, the other a 'feeble-minded' man who was whipped for disrupting the Mass by raising women's skirts over their heads at the moment of consecration.[14] Whatever Sir Thomas's physical role in these events, the burning of books and the torturing and execution of heretics, potentially in their own homes, meant that Margaret and the whole More family were right at the centre of events and at the forefront of the changes happening all over Europe. They also had a front-row seat to events that were unfolding at the English court, and which were going to change their own lives immensely: The King's Great Matter.

Chapter 7

Reformation

1530

When Henry VIII made Sir Thomas chancellor, he did so because the cardinal had been unable to make the king's demands a reality. It was around 1527 that the king decided that he should replace Catherine of Aragon as his wife and queen. She had failed to provide an heir and had not conceived a child in nearly a decade. She was now too old to give him the heir that he so dearly wanted and, for the sake of his throne, needed in order to pass his crown to the next generation of the Tudor dynasty.

This, however, was not an easy request for anyone to fulfil, and despite Cardinal Wolsey's efforts with the papacy, legal cases, diplomacy with the rest of Europe, and trying to persuade Catherine to give up her throne in favour of taking the veil as a nun, he had been unable to secure the divorce that Henry needed, and so he was deposed, replaced by a more friendly, and who Henry hoped would be a less deferential person when it came to the papacy, a lay-person: Sir Thomas More.

Sir Thomas found the job just as difficult as his predecessor did, however, and to make things more complicated, the king had fallen for one of Catherine's ladies-in-waiting, a young noblewoman named Anne Boleyn. She was a member of the

Duke of Norfolk's family and was a follower of the new reforms. She had introduced Henry, through various literature and by inviting preachers to court who were reformist leaning, to the Protestant teachings that suggested that the king, not the pope, and not the priests who served the papacy, should be in charge of the kingdom entirely, and that the authority of the pope should come secondary to his own. For Henry, this was excellent news, and was an idea which helped him in all sorts of ways: financial as now monies that previously went to the pope would come into the royal coffers; his authority would be bolstered and he would be able to make decisions that previously would have been made by the pope in Rome; and, most importantly of all, he would have final say in the granting of a divorce for himself and Queen Catherine.

And so Henry ordered Sir Thomas to split the country from Rome, that the 'Church of England' would be his domain, and that his divorce from Catherine would be finalised so he could marry Anne. This seemed like a simple request by Henry, especially as he was, in his view, supreme head of the church and ruler of England, but Thomas and others in his government struggled to put this in place. In 1529, parliament had reinstated *Praemunire*, a clause in law that made it a crime to say that anyone was above the king's authority, even the pope, but even so there were many, Sir Thomas among them, who were set against this and still maintained support for the papal authority.

Clergymen who supported the king's cause sent a letter to Pope Clement VII in 1530, asking him once again to annul Henry's marriage. Sir Thomas refused to sign this letter, and the pope responded in January 1531, threatening Henry with excommunication should he remarry without papal approval. The pope's allies in court, Sir Thomas, Bishop John Fisher and William Warham, the Archbishop of Canterbury, all fought to keep the papal authority intact, but at the convocation of Canterbury, on 11 February 1531, the senior clergy all accepted the king's supremacy by giving Henry VIII the title of 'singular protector, supreme lord, and even, so far as the law of Christ allows, supreme head of the English church and clergy'.[1] Bishop John Fisher and some other clergy had refused to agree to the title.

All this led to, on 16 May 1532, Thomas More resigning his position as chancellor and stepping away from court life. He had found his position to be untenable, and his views incompatible with the actions the king wanted him to take. William Roper tells us in detail about how he came to make the decision to resign:

> But, Sir Thomas More, in process of time, seeing the King fully determined to proceed forth in the marriage of Queen Anne [...] Nevertheless, doubting lest further attempted after should follow, which – contrary to his conscience, by reason of his office, he was likely to be put unto – he made suit unto the Duke of Norfolk, his singular dear friend, to be a means to the King that he might, with his grace's favour, be discharged of that chargeable [burdensome] room of the Chancellorship. wherein, for certain infirmities of the body, he pretended himself unable any longer to serve.[2]

At the age of 54, More was an elder statesman of the court by that point, and him claiming infirmity and wanting to retire would have been a natural progression. However, coming when it did, his stepping down from public office so completely and suddenly did cause a few ripples in court circles. His resignation was, despite this, accepted by the king in good grace and Thomas took himself back to Chelsea, to spend time in his study and with his family. While immediately this change in circumstances and removal of responsibilities must have been a relief, his reluctance to completely and committedly take the king's side in his quest for an annulment and a separation from the papal authority, was something that would go on to have much more far-reaching effects.

At court, his position had been so prominent that when he took a step back in that manner, it had the appearance that he was perhaps going against the king's wishes, and this may have given an impression of weakness to Henry and his new religious policies. Thomas, while not high-born or able to wield any power through birth, had built a circle of influence around him, and coming up as he had done against the reformers at court, his lack of support for the king could have signalled an effective rebellion against the king's religious reforms and his quest for a divorce from Queen Catherine, with Thomas and the others, such as Bishop John Fisher, as figureheads for the cause. By removing himself from Henry's side, Thomas highlighted the growing chasm between his and the king's position on the roles of the church, papacy and crown.

Thomas's resignation also had wide-ranging ramifications for the family. The home at Chelsea that, as Erasmus described was at the time home to three generations of the More family, was grand and required large quantities of money and staff to keep it running under Alice's capable supervision. The house had become a hub, and Thomas was proud to be able to provide for all his children, grandchildren, and extended household and family members. By stepping down from court and from his role as chancellor, Thomas gave up a very lucrative salary as well as the ability to provide work for some of his relations, including William Roper, through his contacts and influence. Roper again gives us an account of the distress this caused them all:

> After he had thus given over the Chancellorship, and placed all his gentlemen and yeomen with bishops and noblemen, and his eight watermen with the Lord Audley, that in the same office succeeded him – to whom also he gave his great barge – then, calling us all that were his children unto him, and asking our advice how we might now, in this decay of his ability (by the surrender of his office so impaired that he could not, as he was wont, and gladly would, bear out the whole charges of them all himself) and thenceforth be able to live and continue together as he wished we should. When he saw us silent, and in that case not ready to show out opinions to him 'Then I will,' said he, 'show my poor mind unto you. I have been brought up', quoth he, 'at Oxford, at an Inn of Chancery, at Lincoln's Inn and also in the king's court, and so forth from the lowest degrees to the highest, and yet have I in yearly revenues at this present left me little above an hundred pounds by the year, so that now must we hereafter, if we like to live together, be contented to become contributories together.'[3]

The financial strain, and the giving up of his barge, which was his main form of transport to and from the City of London along the Thames, must have been a massive upheaval for the whole family, and with the loss of the links to the court, the rest of the family would have been worried about the future too. As Thomas had only bought leases for his properties, he did not have a large amount of personal wealth, and aside from his personal effects, collection of books and the furniture of his home at Chelsea, the family were going to have to be frugal in order to maintain their lifestyles. Above all else, the family wished to stay together, and Roper quotes Thomas, asking that should their efforts at frugality fail:

> then may we yet with bags and wallets, go a begging together, and hoping that for pity some good folk will give us their charity, at every man's door to sing Salve Regina and so still keep company and be merry together.[4]

Margaret and William were, at the time of his resignation, expecting their fourth child, and while William was installed as a member of parliament his work through Lincoln's Inn was also an important income for the household. They were lucky that they had their other properties to use if they did need to live away from Chelsea, and Eltham particularly was close enough to London that William would be able to maintain his position at parliament.

It was around this time that William and Margaret commissioned their very own miniature portraits from Holbein. It may have been as a way for William particularly to step out from behind his father-in-law, as in the portrait William is shown wearing a safe outfit, one that would not particularly give clues about his religion or affiliation. He was still a member of parliament, and needed to keep his position to enable the family to maintain their standard of living. Margaret on the other hand is not as subtle, pictured with her prayer book in her hand and with a full, Spanish-style hood. These were similar to those worn by Queen Catherine, and completely different to fashions being worn by the newer ladies at court, such as Anne Boleyn. These portraits may well have been an attempt for William and Margaret to be seen as separate, but their allegiance was still clearly with Sir Thomas.[5]

The More family were, therefore, able, by the work of the whole family pulling together, to maintain their lifestyle for the short term, and continue on with what Sir Thomas, and probably the rest of the family, hoped would be a peaceful retirement among his books and grandchildren. However, very quickly, things started to change at court, and even in his rural idyll, Thomas could not avoid being caught up in the upheavals.

In the August of 1532, William Warham, the Archbishop of Canterbury and long-time friend and ally of Thomas, died. This left the see of Canterbury vacant and Henry VIII saw his opportunity to appoint Thomas Cranmer, a reformist-leaning clergyman and an ally of the Boleyn family, into the post. The king wrote to the pope requesting his appointment, and while the pope required an oath of allegiance from any appointee, Cranmer refused to take it seriously. The act of *Praemunire* alone would have made this oath a crime, but he outright stated that he would not accept the oath, merely accept the appointment. Once he officially became the Archbishop of Canterbury, under Henry VIII's new rules, he had the authority to annul the king's marriage to Queen Catherine, and Henry was free to marry Anne. The pair were married in January 1533, technically before the annulment was confirmed in May of 1533. On 1 June, wasting no time, Henry VIII introduced Anne as his new queen, in an extravagant ceremonial coronation at Westminster Abbey. Anne was already pregnant with their first child, Elizabeth, and was presented as the rightful queen by Henry who wanted the whole business of his divorce left behind, to focus on the future, his new wife and the potential heirs that she promised. It was from this point that we can see events start to spiral away from Sir Thomas's control, and bring the whole More family under scrutiny for their beliefs. Their loyalties were questioned at the same time as Sir Thomas's, and the whole household was placed under investigation for the same things. The first event that caused problems was Queen Anne's coronation.

When the coronation was announced, Sir Thomas was invited to attend, along with Dame Alice. There would have been large-scale celebrations at court and in parliament, and it is likely that Margaret, William and the other More siblings would have also been expected to participate in the festivities. However, despite offers of clothes to wear and accommodation from friendly courtiers, and even personal intervention by the bishops of Durham, Bath and Winchester for him to accompany them in the processions, Sir Thomas and Lady More did not attend the coronation of Queen Anne. The reasons he gave, according to Roper, were ones of conscience. Roper insinuates that if Sir Thomas had attended the coronation it would have signified his acceptance of the marriage as legitimate, and that went against his beliefs:

For some there by that by procuring your lordships first at the coronation to be present, and next to preach for the setting forth of it, and finally to write books to all the world in defence thereof, are desirous to deflower you. And when they have deflowered you then will they soon not fail to devour you. Now my lords ... it lieth not in my power but that they may devour me, but God being good Lord, I will provide that they shall never deflower me.[6]

In short, he accuses the bishops of not being true to their beliefs, of giving up their purity, and of allowing this to happen to themselves by supporting something that should not be permitted to take place.

Roper goes into detail about this reasoning, suggesting that the story was at least told to him so he was very familiar with it, if in fact he was not indeed present when the discussion about attendance at the coronation was discussed by Sir Thomas and the rest of the family. It is, therefore, a reasonable assumption that Margaret was also present at these discussions and may well have ventured her own opinion. Although we have no way of telling what that opinion may have been, Roper's recollection appears to show the vehemence with which Sir Thomas believed that by not attending, he was ensuring his conscience was indeed clear.

By not attending though, Sir Thomas opened himself up to more anger and suspicion. It had been very important to Henry that everyone attend and accept Anne as queen. Therefore, a high-profile figure such as Sir Thomas refusing to attend was seen as a snub to the king's authority and this angered the king greatly. Sir Thomas had managed to avoid any potential charges of treason or of defying the king's will, by writing to Henry to express his congratulations to Anne and, on the surface, this was enough to avoid any issues as he seemed to accept the queen's position. However, the public slight was enough to put Henry on edge and Sir Thomas and his family were put into a group of individuals whom the king, and his loyal councillors including Thomas Cromwell, would watch very carefully for any signs of treason or heresy. All of their actions were analysed and assessed for any wrongdoing and should there be any, Henry's councillors were ready to hold them accountable. And so, soon after the coronation, Sir Thomas, alongside a number of other high-profile courtiers, was accused of being supportive of Elizabeth Barton, better known as 'the Holy Maid of Kent'.

Elizabeth Barton was a nun, originally from Canterbury in Kent, who was said to have visions. She would enter a trance-like state and through the visions she received could predict future events and outcomes. Her fame grew as the stories of her correctly predicting deaths, illnesses and other events in people's lives spread across the kingdom, and she became something of a celebrity. She was visited by Archbishop Warham before his death, and by Bishop John Fisher, both of whom believed she was 'filled with the Holy Spirit'; this gave her claims legitimacy as a result. She was invited to London and even spoke in front of Cardinal Wolsey, Sir Thomas and the king himself. But this was the beginning of things turning sour, and when the 'Holy Maid' predicted that, should he leave his true wife, Queen Catherine, then his reign would be in peril:

that in case hys Highnes proceded to th accomplishment of the seid devorce and maried another, that then hys Majestie shulde not be kynge of this Realme by the space of one moneth after, And in the reputacion of God shuld not be kynge one day nor one houre.[7]

Later she prophesied that the king would in fact only live for a month following his marriage to Anne Boleyn and that he would die as the villain of the piece, with his daughter Mary taking the throne instead.

The king was patient with her and did not immediately press for her to be punished for her prophecies and predictions, but, after her predictions did not come to pass and she was mostly discredited, she still commanded loyalty from some of the more staunchly Catholic members of the court, and this did not sit well with Cromwell and the reformers. Cromwell and Archbishop Cranmer both set about attempting to discredit her completely, and eventually, after months of interrogations at their hands, she confessed.[8]

Following this confession and after an Act of Parliament was passed to make speaking of the king's death an act of treason, a warrant was drawn up for the arrest of Elizabeth Barton, a number of her followers and also some of her associates, among whom were Bishop John Fisher and Sir Thomas More. Barton was arrested in January 1534, and following a short trial she was dragged through the streets of London strapped to a wooden board, before being hung. Her head was then struck from her body and it was placed on London Bridge, the only woman to ever be put on display in this manner.[9]

Sir Thomas had been to see her when she was residing at Syon Abbey, and he had also written to her. It was these letters that were the key piece of evidence, as in them he had questioned her about her authenticity and whether indeed she believed her predictions. As Sir Thomas had kept copies of all his correspondence with her, he was able to prove that he was not a supporter of her cause and therefore avoided imprisonment and charges.

All the others named, however, were not so fortunate. Sir Thomas stood by his innocence stating in a letter to Thomas Cromwell that they 'talked no worde of the Kinges Grace or anye great personage ells, no in effecte, of anye man or woman but of her selfe, and my selfe'.[10]

It was not only Sir Thomas who was under suspicion for having consulted with the 'Holy Maid', with the whole family being asked questions and put firmly under suspicion for having supported Elizabeth Barton and her prophecies. Sir Thomas's involvement makes it likely that while she visited her supporters in and around London, she may have come to the Mores and discussed matters with the family, Margaret and William included.

Even if they were able to avoid any charges themselves, there were also the ongoing financial issues that faced the family. The arrests made, and imprisonments of some of their closest friends and acquaintances, Bishop John Fisher being the most prominent, were done through a bill of attainder, and this would have led to all the lands and goods of those imprisoned being forfeit to the crown. The whole family was in danger of losing everything. Even Margaret, who was known for her piety and her loyalty to her father and his group of allies, was suspected of being involved and also, because of her gender, suspected of the same crimes as Barton.

Just a few weeks later, once again a dark cloud hung over the family and their future. This time Sir Thomas was brought before the council to swear his allegiance to the crown, to sign the parliamentary act of succession and to the supremacy of the crown. Less than a year on from his refusal to attend the coronation of Queen Anne, Sir Thomas was once again asked to swear that the king's marriage was lawful and valid, and once again, he refused to do so. He would not and could not declare his support for the annulment of the king's marriage to Queen Catherine, and therefore he refused to sign, swear or accept anything that was put in front of him. His friend and ally, Bishop John Fisher, was called to do the same, and he refused to swear the oath also.

The Oath of Supremacy read:

I, [name] do utterly testifie and declare in my Conscience, that the Kings Highnesse is the onely Supreame Governour of this Realme, and all other his Highnesse Dominions and Countries, as well in all Spirituall or Ecclesiasticall things or causes, as Temporall: And that no forraine Prince, Person, Prelate, State or Potentate, hath or ought to have any Jurisdiction, Power, Superiorities, Preeminence or Authority Ecclesiasticall or Spirituall within this Realme. And therefore, I do utterly renounce and forsake all Jurisdictions, Powers, Superiorities, or Authorities; and do promise that from henchforth I shall beare faith and true Allegiance to the Kings Highnesse, his Heires and lawfull Successors: and to my power shall assist and defend all

Jurisdictions, Privileges, Preheminences and Authorities granted or belonging to the Kings Highnesse, his Heires and Successors or united and annexed to the Imperial Crowne of the Realme: so helpe me God: and by the Contents of this Booke.[11]

The Oath of Succession read:

Ye shall swear to bear faith, truth, and obedience alonely to the king's majesty, and to his heirs of his body of his most dear and entirely beloved lawful wife Queen Anne, begotten and to be begotten, and further to the heirs of our said sovereign lord according to the limitation in the statute made for surety of his succession in the crown of this realm, mentioned and contained, and not to any other within this realm, for foreign authority or potentate: and in case any oath be made, or has been made, by you, to any person or persons, that then ye [are] to repute the same as vain and annihilate; and that, to your cunning, wit, and uttermost of your power, without guile, fraud, or other undue means, you shall observe, keep, maintain, and defend the said Act of Accession, and all the whole effects and contents thereof, and all other Acts and statutes made in confirmation, or for the execution of the same, or of anything therein contained; and this ye shall do against all manner of persons, of what estate, dignity, degree, or condition [whatever] they be, and in no wise do or attempt, nor to your power suffer to be done or attempted, directly or indirectly, any thing or things privily or apartly to the let, hindrance, damage, or derogation thereof, or of any part of the same, by any manner of means, or for any manner of pretence; so help you God, all saints, and the holy Evangelists.[12]

By defying the council and the king, and refusing to sign and acknowledgement or swear any oaths, Sir Thomas was guilty of treason by *Praemunire*, and for this he was arrested, and on 17 April 1534, he was taken to the Tower to await trial for his dissent. His conscience would not allow him to concede, and he was willing to accept the consequences of his actions.

While Sir Thomas may have been content with his course of action, the rest of the More family were in disarray: their father was imprisoned by the king; those who they were friendly with were also imprisoned or had been accused; and their own positions were all under scrutiny, their futures had never been more uncertain. Cromwell and the council approached the family, Margaret included, and demanded that they all swear the oath, unless they wished to join Sir Thomas, their dear husband and father, in the Tower.

Chapter 8

Loyalty

1534

When Sir Thomas was sent to the Tower, the More family were left with choices to make. They were without their figurehead, and under constant suspicion of sharing his views. The whole family were asked to sign and pledge the oaths that Sir Thomas had refused to sign, or they would face the same consequences. Alice and the More siblings, their husbands, wives and children, all agreed and took the Oaths of Supremacy and Succession, and so they remained on the outside, looking in on Thomas as he was held by the king's authority. He refused help from anyone who offered it, and returned everything they sent to make him more comfortable in his accommodation at the Tower. He was not allowed visitors and with so little contact, at times no one knew what his condition was. The family were frantic with worry about Sir Thomas's and their own situations.

When Sir Thomas had left on the morning of 13 April, to attend the meeting with the king's commissioners, no one, least of all him, knew when, or indeed if, he would return. His initial imprisonment saw him lodged at Westminster Abbey, in a small cell, cloistered with the monks. However, after four days of this isolation it was ordered that he should be moved to the Tower, as was more befitting for his situation as a traitor and under attainder. Once at the Tower, he was given lodgings, and the prisoner was expected to pay his own costs of 10 shillings a month for his rooms, and an extra 5 shillings a month to accommodate his servant, John Wood. John had been assistant to Sir Thomas's secretary John Harris, and as such was familiar with the way that Thomas worked, and also the family. Within a few days Wood was granted a pass in and out of the Tower, to serve his master with clean clothes, and to collect the monies for their board and lodging. While he was out of the Tower, he was able to secretly pass letters in and out.[1]

The first letter Sir Thomas appears to have written was addressed to Margaret, intended to be shared with the whole family but written very much with her reception in mind. This would be the way that he chose to correspond with the family, perhaps to be efficient with time, detail and because too many letters would be difficult to smuggle out, or perhaps because it was his intention to keep his beloved Meg in his thoughts while he was imprisoned. He had employed this tactic before in letters sent when he was abroad, or travelling with the court, so this would have been a normal way for him and the family to communicate. Either way, in the letter he tells her, and the rest of the family by proxy, in precise detail what happened to him from the 13 to 17 April, and that now he was well enough, lodged at the Tower. He also goes into great detail about his thoughts, feelings and opinions that had led him to be arrested and imprisoned. This may have been an attempt to console the family, or to persuade them that he had done the 'right thing' in his mind.

A second letter followed shortly after the first. Unlike the first, it was short and to the point, and definitely just for Margaret. It was signed:

Written with a coal by your tender loving father, who in his poor prayers forgetteth none of you all, nor your babes, nor your nurses, nor your good husbands, nor your good husband's shrewd wives, nor your husband's shrewd wife neither, nor our other friends. And thus fare you heartily well for lack of paper.[2]

This short note gives us an insight into the conditions that Sir Thomas was living in, and while he was allowed to have some comforts from home, he was swiftly running out of paper and ink, and called out to Margaret for more. Seeing an opportunity to help her father, Margaret wrote back to her father, but instead of having the letter smuggled in by Wood, she wrote via the Constable of the Tower, knowing full well that the letter would be read. In fact, some historians have said that the letter she sent wasn't even sealed as she was expecting it to be read by Cromwell himself.[3] In it, she explained how she and her husband intended to take the oath, and how she thought that her father should follow in their stead.

When she was brought before the commissioners in person, she utilised her keen intellect to add in the line 'as far as will stand with the law of God'. This had been added in some cases, particularly that of the Carthusian monks, in order to allow them to take the oath within their consciences. This was a risky strategy, as to assume to do this by herself without warning could have been viewed as contemptuous and she risked the same fate as her father. However, the facts were that she was a woman, and as her husband had already proved his loyalty by taking the oath, it was simply accepted that this meant that she was also loyal, and Margaret, therefore, was able to escape repercussions to her actions.

This combination of public shows of loyalty meant that Margaret and the rest of the family were able to continue their normal everyday business. In fact, when Margaret then asked for permission to see Thomas, it was granted in the hopes that Margaret and the others would be able to persuade him to take the oath and then this whole business would be over. Margaret's letter had persuaded Cromwell that if she were able to bring her father into line, then, in the words of John Guy, 'the propaganda value would be huge and Henry's victory complete'.[4]

The rest of the family did get to see Thomas periodically. Dame Alice saw him once when he was initially imprisoned but when she did she was angry with his decisions and, unsurprisingly, emotional with the stress of the situation and chastised him. Roper put down his version of what she said to him:

> What the good year, Master More. I marvel that you, that have always been hitherto taken for so wise a man, will now play the fool to lie here in this close, filthy prison, and be content thus to be shut up amongst the mice and rats, when you might be abroad at your liberty. And with the favour and good will of both the King and his council, if you would but do as all the bishops and best learned of this realm have done. And seeing you have at Chelsea a

right fair house, your library, your books, your gallery, your garden, your orchard and all other necessaries so handsom about you, where you might in the company of me your wife, you children and household be merry, muse what a God's name you mean here still thus fondly to tarry.[5]

Following the visit, she then chose to distance herself from him and did not return, writing to him to let him know family news, and their financial circumstances, but the pair were not in regular contact, and Thomas chose to relay all news through Margaret for the most part.

But this is not to say that Alice was without some concern for her husband and his well-being. In an attempt to help her husband's cause, she wrote to the king to beg for Thomas's release, pleading with him 'to remit and pardon your most grievous displeasure to the saide Sir Thomas' who was 'in greate continuall sicknes of bodye and heuines of harte'.[6] She implored the king to see that Thomas was acting from 'a longe contynued and deep rooted scrupple, and passethe his power to avoid and put away'; his conscience was guiding him and this could not be swayed for his 'scrupple' was too deeply embedded, and this was a quality which, while not excusing his behaviour, did explain it. It could be that Alice hoped that the king's understanding and friendship with Sir Thomas could be drawn upon to give him some understanding of the situation, and therefore he would err on the side of leniency. Unfortunately, the king was not understanding and Sir Thomas remained in the Tower. In fact, things were about to become even worse.

The act of attainder that was put upon him also took away all his worldly goods and possessions, and this included his homes and holdings at Chelsea. All his monies and other assets were seized. Dame Alice was also keen in her letter to emphasise that the family would be 'completely undone' should this property not be returned.[7] As Ackroyd points out, this may well be a little bit of exaggeration on her part, as her own wealth, and the good marriages made by the children did mean that mostly they would not be destitute. Only John, Sir Thomas's youngest son, was left carrying any financial burden, as he was left with responsibility for the debts that Sir Thomas owed the king. There were a few things that he managed to save in the days prior to his imprisonment. Sir Thomas was either being extra cautious, or he was expecting the act of attainder to be passed, and therefore he chose to protect what assets he could. This included signing the Bucklersbury lease over the to the Clements, as up to this point the lease had been held in his name and paid for by him for his stepdaughter and son-in-law, the Clements, and also signing the New Building, Butts Close, over to the Ropers. William and Margaret had been resident there for a while with their family, but now it officially became their property.

The majority of the rest of the family followed Alice's example and distanced themselves from Thomas and his beliefs. William Roper had sworn the oath in parliament and in so doing publicly disassociated himself from critics of the oath and the king's divorce. However, there were some who stayed close to Thomas and supported Margaret in her role as go-between. The Clements, Margaret Giggs and her husband John Clement, did maintain some connection with Thomas while he was in the Tower. They offered accommodation to Margaret when she was visiting her father and wasn't able to get back to the home in

Chelsea, or to Eltham. Although Clement was employed as the king's personal physician, when Sir Thomas and also Bishop Fisher became ill during their time in the Tower, it was John Clement who attended to them personally.

But it was Margaret who was Sir Thomas's main contact with the outside world. Thanks to her intervention, his conditions in the Tower improved immensely; he was allowed to have books and writing implements, his cell was only locked at night and so he was allowed out into the Tower gardens to walk and to the chapel to pray. He even received care packages from his friends and allies, including meat and wine on a weekly basis from Antonio Bonvisi, a well-known trader and banker with close connections with the humanist movement in London. Margaret was his most frequent visitor and throughout 1534 she was found travelling between the Tower and the family home, taking letters, gifts and news from home, and spending time with her ailing father. Sir Thomas was now 56 years old and had started to suffer with various ailments common in men his age. Angina plagued him and caused him pain, kidney stones would occasionally flare, and he suffered with cramps from the damp in his cell. It was Margaret's visits that helped him to stay well and keep up his spirits, as well as his writings, and during his time in the Tower, Margaret was crucial in these too.

In the summer months of 1534, during his imprisonment, when Margaret and he were sharing their visits in prayer and in conversations, Sir Thomas wrote profusely, and his main work was *A Dialogue of Comfort against Tribulation*. Echoing *Utopia* from almost twenty years earlier, it uses the same structure and the work is laid out as a conversation on which the reader is eavesdropping, and the topics are ones of ethics, faith and the maintenance of one's soul. It is a reasonable assumption that Margaret would have had a great deal of influence on this work, given the amount of time that she spent in her father's company at this time, and that she would have been his only sounding board. It is easy to imagine that their conversations would have been the inspiration for him to then write down after she left, then on her next visit they would pick up where they had left off.

This is continued as the structure for other letters that were written during his time in the Tower, but one set of correspondence stands out: a lengthy description of a conversation which is written to Alice Alington, known by historians as 'The Alington Letters'. The Alington letters are written by Margaret, although it is likely that they were a collaboration between Margaret and her father. There is debate about who was the lead author, and whose voice is truly the one heard through the words written. The letter is signed as being Margaret's work, but the structure used and the use of language is so reminiscent of Sir Thomas that it is clear that he had a hand in its construction. The letters open:

> When I came next unto my father after, methought it both convenient and necessary, to shew him your letter. Convenient, that he might thereby see your loving labor taken for him. Necessary, that [since] he might perceive thereby, that if he stand still in this scruple of his conscience (as it is at the leastwise called by many that are his friends and wise) all his friends that seem most able to do him good either shall finally forsake him, or peradventure not be able indeed to do him any good at all.[8]

The content of the letter is complex and covers a number of ethical dilemmas regarding Sir Thomas and his imprisonment. However, there are a number of times in which Margaret tells the reader about how she has implored her father to change his mind, to go back on what he has said and to secure his freedoms, but it is seen that Sir Thomas speaks directly to her to answer these questions about why he cannot do this:

> But Margaret, for what causes I refuse the oath, the thing (as I have often told you) I will never shew you, neither you nor nobody else, except the King's Highness should like to command me. Which If his Grace did, I have ere this told you therein how obediently I have said. But surely, Daughter, I have refused it and do, for more causes than one. And for what causes so ever I refuse it, this am I sure, that it is well known, that of them that have sworn it, some of the best learned before the oath given them, said and plain affirmed the contrary, of some such things as they have now sworn in the oath, and that upon their truth, and their learning then, and that not in haste nor suddenly, but often and after great diligence done to seek and find out the truth.[9]

The complexity of the argument suggests to me that this is a collaboration by father and daughter to attempt to put across Sir Thomas's case. The letter is extremely long and, unlike a more informal family letter, is careful to make sure that each argument is given clear consideration. It is my belief that Margaret wrote the letter, with oversight by her father, as a joint enterprise. By

Margaret writing the letter, and putting her name to it, she was giving her father a voice on the outside. By making it a personal correspondence, the voice that she gave him is an honest and uncomplicated one, without any overt public face or calculated purpose. While many scholars argue that the work is entirely that of her father, I believe that Margaret was more than capable of producing such a work, especially if her father was able to add to it and provide the base conversations. She, by way of these letters, allowed him to put across his point of view, at a time when he was powerless to present this information outside of his prison cell.

Sir Thomas and Margaret continued to see one another frequently throughout the autumn and winter of 1534 and into 1535, until in the spring an addition was made to the Treason Act. This brought in to effect a clause that meant that anyone denying the king's supremacy would be guilty of treason and this would be punishable by death.

Extract of the Treason Act 1535:

> Be it therefore enacted by the assent and consent of our sovereign lord the king, and the Lords spiritual and temporal, and Commons in this present Parliament assembled, and by the authority of the same, that if any person or persons, after the first day of February next coming, do maliciously wish, will or desire, by words or writing, or by craft imagine, invent, practise, or attempt any bodily harm to be done or committed to the king's most royal person, the queen's, or their heirs apparent, or to deprive them or any of them of their dignity, title, or

name of their royal estates, or slanderously and maliciously publish and pronounce, by express writing or words, that the king our sovereign lord should be heretic, schismatic, tyrant, infidel or usurper of the crown ... within six days next after they shall be commanded by our said sovereign lord, his heirs or successors, by open proclamation under the great seal:

... every such offence in any the premises, that shall be committed or done after the said first day of February, shall be reputed, accepted, and adjudged high treason, and the offenders therein and their aiders, consenters, counsellors, and abettors, being lawfully convicted of any such offence as is aforesaid, shall have and suffer such pains of death and other penalties, as is limited and accustomed in cases of high treason.[10]

Sir Thomas was again pressed to take the oath and declare his support for the king's supremacy. This was not something he was willing to do and so he continued to refuse to swear, while still professing his loyalty to the king himself. Thomas Cromwell and the Solicitor General, Sir Richard Rich, attempted to bring the whole issue to a head by making life in the Tower less and less comfortable for the ailing Sir Thomas, as well as for Bishop Fisher who was also still imprisoned. The two men refused to give in, and despite them being repeatedly questioned and having all the extras they had been allowed, even down to their personal servants being removed from the Tower, they both continued to keep their silence on the matter. Margaret was denied access to her father and his health began to deteriorate without his books and her visits to keep his morale up.

One visit from Sir Richard Rich was particularly important, as he engaged in a conversation with Sir Thomas. Here the events are laid out in the minutes from the trial, as printed in 1719:

> Those Examinations being over, Richard Rich, newly made Solicitor General, and afterwards Lord Rich, with Sir Richard Southwell, and Mr. Palmer, Secretary Cromwell's Man, were sent by the King to take away his Books. Rich pretending Friendship to him, and protesting he had no Commission to talk with him about the former Affair of the Supremacy, he put a Case to him thus: If it were enacted by Parliament that Richard Rich should be King, and that it should be Treason in any body to deny it, what Offence it were to contravene that Act? Sir Thomas Moore answered, That he should offend if he said so, because he was bound by the Act; but, that this was casus levis. Whereupon Sir Thomas said, he would propose a higher Case: Suppose it were enacted by Parliament, Quod Deus non sit Deus, and that it were Treason to contravene, whether it were not an Offence to say it according to the said Act? Rich reply'd, yea; but said withal, I will propose a middle Case, because this is too high: The King, you know, is constituted supreme Head of the Church upon Earth; why should not you, Master More, accept him for such? as you would me, if I were made King by the aforesaid Supposition. More answered, the Case was not the same, because, said he, a Parliament can make a King, and depose him; and that every

Parliament Man may give his Consent hereunto, but that a Subject cannot be bound so in the Case of Supremacy.[11]

This conversation was related as such as the trial, which took place on 1 July 1535. The evidence was all laid out and the chancellor, Lord Audley, asked of Sir Thomas:

Presently after the Indictment was read, the Lord Chancellor, and the Duke of Norfolk spoke to him to this effect:

You see now how grievously you have offended his Majesty; yet he is so very merciful, that if you will lay aside your Obstinacy, and change your Opinion, we hope you may obtain Pardon and Favour in his sight. But Sir Thomas stoutly reply'd, 'Most Noble Lords, I have great reason to return thanks to your Honours for this your great Civility, but I beseech Almighty God, that I may continue in the Mind I am in, thro' his Grace, unto Death.'

Throughout the trial the fact that Sir Thomas had refused to take the oath, or to make any sign either way about his views, was the main crux of the argument they had against him:

Attorney. Sir Thomas, tho we have not one Word or Deed of yours to object against you, yet we have your Silence, which is an evident sign of the Malice of your Heart: because no dutiful Subject, being lawfully ask'd this Question, will refuse to answer.

Sir Thomas More. Sir, my Silence is no sign of any Malice in my Heart, which the King himself must Own by my Conduct upon divers Occasions; neither doth it convince any Man of the Breach of the Law.[12]

It was a long time before the trial came to court, with Sir Thomas spending over a year in the Tower beforehand, but the evidence brought by Sir Richard Rich meant that once the trial started Sir Thomas was quickly found guilty and was sentenced to death for treason. The method of execution for treason was to be hung, drawn and quartered, described in the trial minutes as:

That he should be carried back to the Tower of London, by the Help of William Kingston, Sheriff, and from thence drawn on a Hurdle through the City of London to Tyburn, there to be hanged till he should be half dead; that then he should be cut down alive, his Privy Parts cut off, his Belly ripped, his Bowels burnt, his four Quarters sit up over four Gates of the City: and his Head upon London-Bridge.[13]

The method of execution was changed though, after a King's Pardon was received and Thomas and Bishop Fisher were both to be executed by beheading on Tower Hill instead of suffering the full sentence as described above. This was considered a mercy, and was due to Thomas's position in society and the years of service he had given the king. Henry had counted Sir Thomas amongst his friends so perhaps this was an act of kindness by the king; when he was unable to offer his friend a complete pardon, he could offer him a quicker, less painful death.

However, this slight change would have been of little comfort to the family. Following his sentencing, Margaret waited for her father to be escorted back to the Tower. All prisoners took the same route back from Westminster Hall, along the Thames, and entered the Tower walls through a small gate and drawbridge. This is where she waited for him and when he arrived she forced her way past his armed retinue of guards and embraced him. William Roper gives a detailed account of his wife's actions on that day:

> When Sir Thomas More came from Westminster to the Tower again, his daughter, my wife, desirous to see her father, whom she though she should never see in this world after, and also to have his final blessing, gave attendance about the Tower wharf, where she knew he would pass by, before he could enter into the Tower, there tarrying for his coming home. As soon as she saw him, after his blessing on her knees reverently received, she hasting towards him, and without consideration or care of herself, pressing in among the midst of the throng and company of the guard with halberds and bills went round him, hastily ran to him, and there openly, in the sight of all, embraced him, took him about the neck and kissed him.[14]

She held on to him for as long as she was allowed by the guards, and then after being asked to leave, she once more pushed through to give her father one last hug and kiss. He begged her to pray to God for the salvation of his soul and then released her and, without looking back, entered the Tower for the last time.[15]

Sir Thomas wrote one final letter to his daughter on 5 July, and with it he sent his hair shirt so that he would not be seen to be wearing one when he was executed. In his letter, he once again asked her to send on his wishes to her siblings and the extended family, but didn't even mention Alice. It could be that another letter was sent to Alice but that has not survived. The letter he sent to Margaret read:

> Our Lord bless you, my good daughter, and your good husband, and your little boy, and all yours, and all my children, and all my god-children, and all our friends. Recommend me when ye may, to my good daughter Cecily, whom I beseech Our Lord to comfort. And I send her my blessing, and to all her children, and beg her to pray for me. I send her a handkerchief; and God comfort my good son, her husband. My good daughter Dauncey hath the picture in parchment, that you delivered me from my Lady Conyers; her name is on the back of it. Shew her that I heartily pray [for] her, that you may send it in my name to her again, for a token from me to pray for me. I like especially well Dorothy Colly; I pray you be good unto her. I would wit [know] whether that be she you wrote me of; if not, yet I pray you be good to the other as you may, in her affliction, and to my good daughter Joan Aleyn too. Give her, I pray you, some kind answer, for she sued hither to me this day, to pray you to be good to her. I cumber you, good Margaret, much, and I should be sorry if it were to be any longer than to-morrow: for it is St. Thomas's even, and the utas [vigil] of St. Peter; and therefore to-morrow

long I to go to God: it were a day very meet and convenient for me. – I never liked your manner towards me better, than when you kissed me last for I like when daughterly love and dear charity have no leisure to look to worldly courtesy. Farewell, my dear child, and pray for me, and I shall for you, and for all your friends, that we may merrily meet in heaven. I thank you for your great cost. I send now to my good daughter Clement her algorism stone, and send her and my godson, and all hers, God's blessing and mine. I pray you, at time convenient, recommend me to my good son John More; I liked well his natural fashion. Our Lord bless him, and his good wife, my loving daughter, to whom I pray him to be good, as he hath great cause; and if the land of mine come to his hand, he break not my will concerning his sister Dauncey. And our Lord bless Thomas and Austen, and all that they shall have.[16]

On the morning of 6 July, Sir Thomas and Bishop John Fisher, recently made a cardinal by the pope, made their way to the scaffold at Tower Hill. The warrant for their execution had only been signed the night before by the king, just before he left on summer progress, and the news that the execution would take place was only made public in the very early hours of the morning. As a result of this late notice, there was no crowd present for their executions. Some people did manage to come but the audience was small in comparison to other high-profile executions, but this was by design as the king, and Cromwell, did not want to make martyrs out of the bishop and Sir Thomas, so by keeping everything low key, they hoped that this would be avoided, passing almost unnoticed.

It is likely that Margaret did not want to be present at her father's execution. She may have known that it would take place soon, given his letter on the day before, and his sending of his hair shirt; it seems as though Sir Thomas, although maybe not knowing with certainty, knew that he did not have long to wait before his death. He may have asked her in previous visits not to attend, for his sake as much as hers, or it may have been because of the early hour and the short notice, Margaret simply was not able to make the journey to Tower Hill in time.

The only person from the More household present at the execution was Margaret Clement (Giggs). She would have been able to relay the words spoken by Sir Thomas before his execution, in which he asked the gathered, albeit small, crowd to pray for his soul in this world and that he would pray for them in the next world. In his famous quote, meant as a taunt to those who had forced his hand and led him to be executed, he said that he died, 'The King's good servant, but God's first'.[17] Following his death, his body was taken by Margaret Giggs to the Chapel of St Peter ad Vincula to be buried, and his head was taken to London Bridge, to be displayed for all to see, as a warning of what might happen to anyone opposing the king.

Chapter 9

Mortality

1535

Sir Thomas More was dead, and Margaret and the rest of the More family were in disarray. His long imprisonment and the seizure of all his assets had left Alice and the rest of the family still living at Chelsea but with little income, and no direction, unsure of what was now expected of them. With Sir Thomas's death, there was some closure and the family now knew that life as they had known it would never be the same again. Dame Alice left Chelsea, bound for the property she had owned since before her marriage to Sir Thomas, and the children all had to go to their own abodes, either in the city or further afield. All the belongings they had clung on to were either sold to pay the debts that Sir Thomas left behind, or were hastily transported away so as not to be added to the property listing that would be handed over to the crown.

Margaret, William and the children had no choice but to continue with life as normal. Thomas's death shone the light of suspicion on the whole family and with William still working at the court, it was crucial to maintain the status quo. William managed to maintain his position as member of parliament throughout the whole period, and by keeping his head down and accepting all the oaths and acts that were passed, he and his family were able to get through relatively unscathed, pursuing a quiet life after a period of such drama.

It should be said though that this quiet life was not something that Margaret seemed to be worried about. She tried throughout to maintain her father's dignity, and perhaps he had given her instruction during his last days that she felt compelled to carry out. Whatever her motivations, she was not content to leave her father's head to its ignominious fate. As a traitor to the crown, his head went on display, dipped in tar to preserve it against the elements and then impaled on a spike on London Bridge. Heads would normally stay there for a number of weeks, if not months if there were no other executions, before being cast aside, never being reunited with the rest of the body. Margaret was not willing to see this happen, and according to sources including Thomas Stapleton she, finding out that her father's head would be removed, paid the keeper so that she might retrieve it herself:

> [The head] by order of the King, was placed upon a stake on London Bridge, where it remained for nearly a month, until it had to be taken down to make way for other heads ... The head would have been thrown into the river, had not Margaret Roper, who had been watching carefully and waiting for the opportunity, bribed the executioner whose office it was to remove the heads and obtained possession.[1]

She was brought in front of the King's Council, to answer for charges relating to it. What she had done was illegal and therefore she once again risked serious repercussions for her actions. Stapleton tells us:

> Margaret Roper was brought before the King's Council and charged with keeping her father's head as a sacred relic, and retaining possession of his books and his writings. She answered that she had saved her father's head from being devoured by the fishes, and with the intention of burying it; that she had hardly any books and papers but what had been already published, except a very few personal letters, which she humbly begged to be allowed to keep for her own consolation. By the good offices of friends she was released.[2]

It is not clear whether these events actually happened. All the evidence we have in reference to Margaret taking her father's head is in some court records, and the records for the period when this meeting would have taken place no longer exist. However, there is a head in Canterbury, buried in the crypt at St Dunstan's Church with Margaret and her descendants, which would add credence to the story and perhaps show that she did indeed rescue and preserve her father's head.

This was not the last time that Margaret would find herself the focus of legal proceedings. In 1537, less than two years after her father's death, Cromwell again came to suspect her of heresy relating to her father's books and letters. The central focus for Margaret at this time was to ensure that all her father's works were kept for posterity; they were to be preserved with the eventual aim of publishing them. She had enlisted the help of her father's old secretary, John Wood, and with his assistance was collecting letters, manuscripts and anything else that might be useful in preserving her father's ideology. Luckily, Wood still had a lot of Sir Thomas's old papers and in them were the remnants of the great tract-like letters that he had sent to Cromwell and to the king, laying out his views on the supremacy. Also helping her was Margaret Giggs, and this friendship was what would cause Cromwell to become suspicious of her activities.

After the marriage of Henry VIII and Anne Boleyn had ended in Anne's execution in 1536, with no male heir for Henry's troubles, he became more paranoid than ever about the security of his crown and his need for an heir. He was suspicious of anyone in the kingdom who was a potential threat to his crown, and this included the Pole family.

The Poles were known Catholic loyalists, Reginald Pole had been in exile for his faith, but the rest of his family remained in England. In 1537, Geoffrey Pole, Reginald's brother, was questioned by Cromwell and the council about his activities. He was a known associate of Margaret Giggs who had also become known to Cromwell for her own activities. She had taken to, in the description David Knowles gives vividly, disguising herself as a milkmaid 'with a great pail upon her head', and was taking food and other supplies to the last of the monks from the London Charterhouse – which had housed Sir Thomas More – and had remained connected to the More family and refused to take the oath. The monks were housed in Newgate Prison and Margaret Giggs was visiting them regularly incognito, to help them and to aid them in their plight.[3] This had been discovered by Cromwell who, wanting to avoid any further issues with regards to the oath and the supremacy, had covered the whole thing up and attempted to move on instead. However, Geoffrey Pole's testimony named both Margaret Giggs and then Margaret Roper in his circle, and he was forced to confront their actions once again. He stated that he had not only spoken to both of them, but that he had been reading manuscripts by Sir Thomas, and this was not something that Cromwell wanted to continue.[4]

At the time of his death, Sir Thomas's role in the reformation and its happenings was somewhat overshadowed by Bishop Fisher's death at the same time. Cromwell wanted to keep the volume of writing about both men to a minimum and therefore any printing of Sir Thomas's works was worrying to him.

Margaret could see how important her father's work was and would be to future readership. She had, through her own printed work and through seeing what her father had been able to achieve through his publications, experienced how effective the printed word was in spreading ideas and also in keeping things alive long after the person who wrote them was gone. So she gathered together all his published, and some of his unpublished, writings and letters, with the sole aim of publishing them.

She was known to be doing this, and Cromwell summoned her to the King's Council once again, to answer for her actions. According to Cresacre More, who was Margaret's great-nephew, Cromwell once again took her gender into consideration, and because she was a woman she 'was not so hardly dealt withal, but only threatened very sore … [and] was at last sent home to her husband'.[5] Once again, we can see the attitudes of the time, that Margaret was 'sent home to her husband', and her actions were not considered to be as punishable as a man's would have been. Maybe this is lucky, as Margaret was determined to carry out her plans and with them came a lot of risk.

Perhaps because of all these brushes with the authorities at court, or perhaps she simply wanted to concentrate on her work and her children, it would appear that following these events, the Ropers spent more time out of London, at the Roper homes in Eltham and particularly in Place Hall, Canterbury. Around this time also, the last of the lands that had once been the home of the More family were taken from Dame Alice and while she still had her own properties, she was left with a small pension of £20 per year (approximately £8,500 per year in today's money). Therefore, the Ropers may have felt that for their own stability, it was better to take themselves to the more comfortable surroundings offered in Kent.

Not much can be seen today of their homes; however, small clues have been left behind that suggest that their homes would have been very comfortable. Well Hall, in Eltham was a large collection of buildings, and today only the Tudor barn survives.[6] This was built c.1525, and so would have been very familiar to Margaret, William and the family. In Canterbury, the Roper Gate still stands opposite St Dunstan's Church, and would have marked the entrance to Place Hall where the family lived.[7] The opulent design of the gate and of the barn in Eltham both give us a hint at the stylish and relatively lavish buildings that would have formed their homes.

The homes at Eltham and Canterbury were a sanctuary from what was happening at court and in London society. Immediately after the execution of Sir Thomas, the court continued as normal. However, things unravelled quickly for the new queen, Anne Boleyn; after suffering a miscarriage in early 1536, the king determined that their marriage had failed before it had even begun and she was beheaded in May 1536. Henry remarried swiftly, just a matter of days after Anne Boleyn was executed, and in 1537 Jane Seymour gave the king the male heir he so longed for, before succumbing to puerperal fever, better known as 'childbed' fever, or an infection which took hold following what was described as a very long and arduous birth. Jane died on 24 October 1537, and once again the court, and the king, were unsure of what would happen next. Henry VIII now had three children, born to three different queens, and his only heir was an infant. He set about finding another wife, but now he was 46 years old, overweight and suffering from a number of ailments such as gout, and his ulcerous leg made it harder and harder for him to be mobile. Henry, therefore, sought a match that would not only secure him more heirs, but might also make for a more peaceful future for England, and so the deal was done that his fourth wife would be Anne of Cleves, the sister of William, elector of Cleves, and one of the most powerful leaders in the new Protestant areas of Europe. This alliance was supposed to form a foundation for England away from Catholic France and Spain, and make England more secure as a result.

Anne and Henry were married on 6 January 1540, but their marriage only lasted six months before the king sought yet another divorce, and remarried for a fifth time, to a teenaged Catherine Howard. This marriage lasted only a few months, before she was found guilty of adultery and was beheaded, meeting the same fate as her cousin Anne Boleyn before her. Henry knew he still needed to produce another heir and so he took a sixth wife, Katherine Parr, in 1543. Katherine was a known reformer, was well educated, and was the daughter of Maud Parr, a former lady-in-waiting to Queen Catherine of Aragon, after whom she may well have been named. Katherine Parr was born in 1512, and while there is no evidence of her being present at court, she may well have shared lessons with a young Princess Mary, or at least her own upbringing may have been influenced by Queen Catherine's education of the princess and, by extension, Margaret's and her siblings' experience at the 'More School'. Katherine Parr set about reconciling the king with his children, and employed tutors for Princess Elizabeth, who was 10 years old when they married. She employed Roger Ascham, John Christopherson, John Cheke, Richard Cox and others who had been influenced by the humanist way of educating women, and who used the examples of Margaret and her sisters as how to educate the young princess.[8] She also requested that Anthony Cooke become tutor to a young Edward VI. He would go on to educate his own daughters to a very high standard, and they would become as well known as the More children for their abilities.

Away from the scandals and events at court, Margaret also focused her attention on her own circumstances and work, and on caring for and educating her family of young children. She made it her work to keep her father's memory and wishes alive and because of this, education became the main priority for the Roper family. All the children received the same forms of instruction that Margaret and her siblings had previously, and even additional lessons in some cases.

It is probable that, due to their position in court being different to that of her father's, Margaret would have tutored the children herself for much of the time. The Ropers, while not being isolated from society completely, were not as well liked as they had been when Sir Thomas was alive. They still maintained links with the extended family, and with the humanist movement, but they were mostly restricted to their homes in Kent; as such they were not as well connected and this would have limited the numbers of people willing, able or even known to them to become tutors. Unlike Sir Thomas, who had a steady stream of visitors and people willing to come and work and stay with him, this was not the case for Margaret, William and their children.

The older children, Elizabeth and Margaret particularly, were old enough to have remembered their grandfather and possibly to have started their tuition while living in the house at Chelsea, and therefore it is possible that not only did they receive the full benefit of a 'More School' education but that Sir Thomas may have, in the same way that he oversaw the education of his own children, taken an active interest. Mary (born *c.*1529) and Thomas (*c.*1533) may have been slightly too young to have received any tuition, but the influence of their grandfather definitely would have been present and it is likely also that they and their cousins, of which there were many, would have been educated together, taking time in each other's houses and when a particular tutor was employed by them. The 'More School' ethos, therefore, continued through Margaret and her siblings, and through the employment of tutors to encourage a varied curriculum.

Margaret did her best to emulate the education that she and her siblings had received, with a focus on the classical languages and scholars, and on religious texts. She made requests to many noted scholars to come to tutor her children, most notable of whom was Roger Ascham, who while he turned down the request, and eventually went on to tutor the Princess Elizabeth, he later in a letter from 1554, commended Mary on her skills stating 'by your own efforts you excel in this very learning'.[9] Ascham's particular focus was on Latin and Greek, and this was something that Mary in particular would go on to be exceptionally skilled in, receiving tuition above and beyond that of her mother.

After Roger Ascham refused, Henry Cole was brought in as a replacement.[10] Cole, unlike Ascham who was known to have reformist Protestant beliefs, was a Catholic scholar and therefore was viewed as a safe option for the family. While he did not have the reputation that Ascham did as a scholar, he appears to have been a good fit for the children, and stayed with them for a number of years. He was a clergyman as well as a scholar, and during the reign of Mary I went on to take on the role of Vicar of the Spiritualities, one of a few who were responsible for royal religious ceremonies.

While Margaret busied herself with the home and the children, more drama was about to hit the family, as Giles Heron, the husband of her younger sister Cecily, was charged with treason. What had started as a quarrel with one of his tenants ended with him given no trial to speak of, attainted leaving his family destitute, taken to the Tower, and then disembowelled at Tyburn.[11] Cecily and the children were left with nothing and Cecily even appealed directly to the king, begging him for help: 'We now have no friends in the world to help us, but only depend on the King's Majesty's goodness.'[12]

The king did take pity on them of sorts, by paying some of the family's debts to tutors and other staff, and then giving them a small amount for food and clothing, but Cecily and the children were left to fend for themselves. This must have been frightening for Margaret, who was still quietly trying to bring together her father's works so that they might be published. However, this show of force against a member of her family, so soon after her father's execution and her own close calls with the king's authority, must have made her think twice about continuing with her work, and certainly to put thoughts of publishing to one side.

Another few years passed for the family, and they seemed to once again be settling down, when, in late 1543, royal guards arrived to arrest William. He was charged with plotting against Thomas Cranmer, the Archbishop of Canterbury and when investigations, led by the archbishop himself, dug deeper, most of the male members of the More family were also arrested: William Dauncey and John Clement, Margaret's brothers-in-law; her brother John; her nephew John Elrington; and her children's tutor Henry Cole. All were followers of the humanist movement and what was coming to be known as 'the old faith', Catholicism. John Clement and Henry Cole were quickly freed, found by Cranmer's investigation to have done nothing wrong. William Dauncey and John More were both pardoned, but were required to swear the oath or face treason charges. William was the only one remaining in prison, and he was kept there in solitary confinement for four months and then fined £100 on his release.[13] Once again Margaret and William had come close to disaster because of their faith.

What made matters worse for Margaret was that she was pregnant again. She was 39 years old and even today this would be considered of higher risk; in the Tudor period the stakes were even higher. William would probably have been released from his incarceration before Anthony's birth in the spring of 1544, and Margaret would have had the support of not only her sisters but her daughters also. In 1544, Elizabeth was 21 years old, Mary was

15, so seeing their mother go through a pregnancy would have been an experience for them as much as for her. Unfortunately, unlike earlier confinements, Margaret did not have the support of Alice, her stepmother, as she and William had had a disagreement about some of Sir Thomas's estate and this had led her to remove herself from her stepchildren's lives to live peacefully with her small pension granted by the king. So, as Margaret entered her confinement surrounded by the female members of her immediate family, she was excited about this fresh start, but still worried about what the future might bring next.

Perhaps it was the stress on her body of a late child, or the worry from her husband's incarceration and the suspicion cast on virtually every single member of her remaining family, but the exertion took its toll on Margaret and she fell ill. While it is not clear exactly when she became sick, and we do not know the cause of her death, coming so close to Anthony's birth it can be suggested that a complication to do with the birth or thereafter may have been the cause. Guy also asserts that there were cases of the plague in London at the time, and this may well have been the cause.[14] Whatever the matter was, the family was not expecting her death, and when she died quite suddenly around Christmas 1544 it was a shock to everyone. She was taken to the Chelsea Old Church where her father had built his memorial all those years ago, and his head was laid next to her in the crypt.

She left behind her five children, one just a baby, her story mirroring her mother's and setting the household on a path of yet more uncertainty. Immediately after her death, her belongings were distributed according to her wishes: her father's letters and hair shirt were given to Margaret Giggs for safe keeping, her rosary and pendant as well as her collection of Sir Thomas's books were gifted to her daughter Mary for her further study. William received two silver bowls, known as 'Sir Thomas More's bowls', to be held for their youngest son, Anthony, but nothing directly for himself. Perhaps this was because of the disruption that he had caused over the years, or perhaps she already knew that all her worldly goods would be going to him by law and so her legacy to him did not need to be specified.[15]

Chapter 10

Legacy

1545

Margaret's sudden death in 1544 was a shock to all around her, and it took a long time for the family to regain what could be considered stability. With Sir Thomas's death, and then Dame Alice separating herself from the family, Margaret had taken on the role as head of the family. With William and the children, the Ropers and the Clements had become a solid unit and to lose the matriarch would have been a blow.

As well as leaving a gap in their lives, Margaret left behind a legacy of her writing and scholarly work. She had spent the decade since her father died collecting, collating and preserving his works, and she had continued to study, to teach her children and to continue in her father's footsteps as much as she could manage. Margaret's work to preserve the writings of her father was of such importance to her, that when she died William could not ignore it. It had been his wife's focus since the death of her father, and Sir Thomas had also had a massive impact on his own life too. William had spent decades in the More home and had been mentored in both his legal and political careers, as well as in how to raise a family and in his faith. Sir Thomas had been the lynchpin of the family, and so following Margaret's death he attempted to pick up the project on her behalf. This culminated when from about 1550 onwards he started to compile *A Man of Singular Virtue: Being a Life of Sir Thomas More by his son-in-law William Roper.* The book was finally published in 1626 in Paris, after his own death, but he had worked on the book for many years, compiling letters and writing at length about everyday life, the key events of the life of his father-in-law, and also about his beliefs and what he stood for.[1]

In order to complete the book, William required access to the letters, documents and manuscripts that his father-in-law had written, and which had been retrieved and preserved by his wife. They were distributed amongst family members on her death, and this may have been an act of preservation in itself. After her husband's incarceration in 1543–1544, Margaret may well have been concerned that, should the entire collection be found in his possession, he would be imprisoned once again and her children, in particular her youngest child, Anthony, would be left entirely alone in the world. Instead, she separated the collection between trusted family members who would have good reason to hold them and may be, therefore, able to avoid any punishments, or who were willing to take the risk of holding them for her, as was the case of Margaret Giggs. When William needed to refer to these texts in order to complete his work, he needed to see them and would have had to request access from Margaret Giggs and others. Margaret's diligence ensured his work, and that of the many later generations of historians, could continue.

In the decades following there were a number of biographies of Sir Thomas More, including one by his great-great-grandson Cresacre More. Other biographers included Thomas Stapleton and Nicholas Harpsfield; even Shakespeare wrote a play of St Thomas's life. All these works called upon William's writings and the collections that had been preserved by Margaret and her family.

Elsewhere in his life, William also continued to honour his wife in other ways. He did not remarry, instead focusing on his work in parliament; he continued to be a member of parliament up to the accession of Mary I. When Henry VIII died in 1547, William continued to serve his son and heir, Edward VI, when others, including his brother-in-law, John Clement, went into exile. When Queen Mary I took the throne in 1553 he was made prothonotary of the Court of the King's Bench, a position he was allowed to keep when her sister Elizabeth acceded in 1558. From 1554–1555 he served as High Sheriff of Kent, and he was an active member of local society in Kent throughout his life. However, primarily William Roper dedicated the rest of his life to working towards his family goals, bringing up his children and honouring his wife's wishes to carry out work on behalf of her father.

When William Roper died in 1578 he was approximately 81 years old. He requested that he be buried next to his wife in Chelsea Old Church; however, the tenants of Chelsea Manor at that point were the Paulets and they refused him access to the crypt in order to be interred. He was, therefore, taken to the Roper family tomb at St Dunstan's Church in Canterbury and their son Thomas had his mother's remains moved to be with William's in St Dunstan's also. A new chapel was built by the family and in the crypt an alcove was constructed specially to house the head, thought to be that of Sir Thomas More, which Margaret had lying in her tomb with her in Chelsea.[2] New monuments were erected to those buried in the crypt. In his catalogue of *Antiquities of Canterbury (1640),* William Somner gives us a detailed description of the tombs that were present.

> In a side Chapell or Chancell here belonging to the Ropers and wherein anciently two chaplains were of that family maintained to sing for the soules of such of the family as were dead and for the prosperity of their heires living, and had given and allowed to each of them 8 lib. per annum for their salary or wages, beside a little tenement, next the mansion place of the Ropers, for their habitation you may finde these monuments.

> Pray for the soule of John Roper Esquire, sometime generall attourney to our Sovereigne Lord King Hen. 8. and Prygnatory of the bench of our said Sovereigne Lord, and for the soule of Jane his wife, daughter of St John Hyneux Knight chief Judge of England, which John died the 7th day of April in the yeare of the incarnation of Ihu' Christ 1524. on whose soules and all his antecessors soules Jhu' have mercy, Amen.

> Here lies the venerable man William Roper the squire, son and heir of the erstwhile John Roper the squire and Margaret the wife of the same, the daughter of the late Thomas Mori, a high soldier, once chancellor of England, very learned in Greek and Latin letters, who he succeeded his father in the office of prothonotary of the supreme court of the Royal Banci, in which he had served faithfully for 54

years, leaving the same office to his eldest son Thomas. He was munificent at home and abroad, gentle, merciful, a staff of the imprisoned, the oppressed, and the poor. He had two sons and three daughters by his wife Margareta (who was the only one he had), of whom he saw grandchildren and great-grandchildren in his lifetime, he lost his wife in his manhood, he lived as a widower and [mourned] his wife for 33 years. desired by all in good old age, on the fourth day of the month of Jan. In the year of Christ the Savior, 1577, at the true age of his 82nd year.[3]

If you visit the chapel today, although the tombs themselves are still present, the inscriptions are all gone so it is impossible to tell which tomb belongs to William and Margaret. However, beneath the chapel in the crypt, archaeologists have confirmed that there is a head, encased in lead and still sitting in its specially constructed alcove.

As well as William, Margaret's children would also go on to leave their own mark and their achievements were all inspired and in part due to the work and dedication of their mother. After Margaret's unexpected death, William swiftly arranged marriages for his eldest daughters to local landowners in Kent. However, Mary, Thomas and Anthony were all too young to marry immediately and so stayed with their father and their tutors for longer. Mary eventually married Stephen Clarke, but he died early in their marriage, and she remarried in 1556 to James Basset, an MP like her father and a well-connected landowner in Devon and Cornwall. She, however, remained at court a lot of the time, as a lady-in-waiting to Queen Mary and spent a lot more time working on translations, particularly of her grandfather's works. Her translation of *De tristitia Christi* by Sir Thomas was included in one of the earliest compilations of More's works, printed *c*.1557 by her relative William Rastell, thanks to Mary's influence as a member of the closest circle to the queen.

Her older son, Thomas, would become a member of parliament, following in the career footsteps of his father. Educated at Lincoln's Inn, just like his father and grandfather before him, he became an MP in 1553 under the government of Queen Mary, when his Catholicism was no longer an impediment. He married well, and had ten children, keeping the Roper estates in Canterbury and Eltham, building the Roper chapel above the family crypt, and interring his mother and father there alongside his grandfather's head. He and his children were loyal to their More heritage, and an inscription dedicated to Sir Thomas was placed in the church during the reign of Queen Elizabeth I, despite the risks that implied; Sir Thomas, and the faith that he represented were still very much against the laws of the land, and to show such loyalty was dangerous and risked serious repercussions. Their younger son, Anthony, married a local Kent landowner's daughter, Anne Cotton, and produced eight children. He was a local politician also, and was Lord Mayor of Farningham where he left a charitable trust in his name upon his death in 1597.[4]

Following in Margaret's footsteps, Mary went on to publish her own translations, including a translation of *Ecclesiastical History* by Eusebius which she started shortly after her mother's death and published in 1553, when Queen Mary I took the throne. The work was dedicated to Queen Mary, and was praised by Catholic scholars at the time for both the accuracy of the translation and also Mary's own notations and stylistic interpretations of the text which she adds throughout. Like her mother before her, she saw through the text and could extract both deeper meaning and also political message through clever use of language in translation.[5]

According to the chronicler and biographer of Sir Thomas More, Nicholas Harpsfield, Mary also produced translations of other classical scholars such as Socrates and Theodoretus, although no copies of this work exist. Only one original copy of her *Ecclesiasticus Historicae* survives, and that currently resides in the British Library, alongside her mother's works.[6] Her works, as well as Margaret's before her, were a key feature in the Catholic counter-reformation movement in England and even further afield, and Mary's writings were a major pillar in Queen Mary's change back to Catholicism in England.

With Mary also, the tradition of education would continue. She had two sons, and they would have a full Morean schooling thanks to their mother. Her first son, Phillip, was named after his godfather, none other than King Phillip II of Spain, husband of Queen Mary I of England. He trained as a lawyer at Lincoln's Inn, but was expelled due to his faith. Her second son, Charles, was connected with prominent Catholics also, including well-known Jesuit priest Robert Persons, who when writing to recommend Charles for a place at the English College in Rome wrote that he was 'a youth of an illustrious and wealthy family and the great-grandson of Sir Thomas More with talent, manners, virtues worthy of himself and his ancestors'.[7]

Margaret and William's children, and their grandchildren, were all devout Catholics. Some of them were cast out of society, exiled, or punished in the harshest ways for their beliefs, yet they continued to follow the teachings of their parents. This tradition of teaching and education can be traced directly back to Sir Thomas and his influence on Margaret and her sisters. It stretched further than just the More family lines. By demonstrating what a positive impact education had on women, Sir Thomas set in motion a change that could be seen throughout England.

While this was mostly limited to more affluent families, particularly royalty and nobility, we see a shift towards women and girls being given a wider, more classical education, better equipping them for life in a cosmopolitan court. Prime examples are princesses Elizabeth and Mary, and Katherine Parr and others of that generation who learnt languages and studied classical religious texts. As the century moved on there were other scholarly women such as Elizabeth Hardwick and Mary Ward, who would go on to make lasting impressions of their own in education.[8]

The Scholemaster, written by Roger Ascham, was published in 1570. It was a guide for parents on how to educate their children, and like Juan Luis Vives's *The Education of a Christian Woman* before it, it gave guidance specifically on the education of girls. His experiences of teaching Princess Elizabeth and his time spent in the company of like-minded educators meant that this work was radical in some of the content. He refers throughout to 'the chylde' rather than the boy or girl, suggesting that the advice he gives is applicable to both genders. While it is expressly meant for 'the private bringing up of youth in gentlemen and noble men's houses', the proliferation of print meant that anyone who could read it, could use the information he gave.[9] The work was published posthumously and was printed complete with the covering letter from his wife, very well written and introducing her husband to the reader through the letter addressed to Sir William Cecil:

> Syr, move me of right to offer this my late husbands M. Aschams worke unto you. For well remembryng how much all good learnyng oweth unto you for defense therof, as the University of Cambridge, of which my said late husband was a member, have in choosing you their worthy Chancellor acknowledged, and how happily you have spent your time in such studies & caried the use therof to the right ende, to the good service of the Queenes Majestie ...[10]

In the general population too, the rates of literacy amongst both men and women began to grow. Statistics show that literacy rates were around 7 per cent of the population in 1450. This rose considerably to around 16 per cent by 1550.[11] More literature was produced to appeal to a female readership as printing presses became more common across Europe; they reproduced romances, poetry and stories that appealed to every walk of life. The English works of Chaucer were reproduced in huge numbers, the courtly love stories that had come out of medieval France were all immensely popular, and translations of religious and classical texts were perennial favourites.

But it was the original examples set by Sir Thomas and his 'More School', and the outcomes embodied by Margaret particularly that showed what could be achieved by an educated woman; as such, Margaret herself, and not just her father, can be described as an inspiration to a whole generation of women who came after. The longevity of this was lengthened by her work with her daughter, and Mary's continuation of this example again showed how a good, pious, learned woman could contribute and be seen in a positive light.

It must be acknowledged though that this was not a trend that continued. Into the seventeenth and eighteenth centuries, while literacy and schooling in general was accepted as a part of a girl's upbringing, and that women should be able to read, write and have a certain amount of knowledge, it was not accepted that women should be educated, and certainly not to the same extent or level that a boy would be. The path that had appeared before women and girls in the humanist renaissance, thanks to Sir Thomas More and his followers, was stalled and women started to take their more common place in the home.

Margaret and her fellow learned women, her daughter Mary included, took something of a backseat to their male counterparts. William Roper's biography was the work that was acknowledged and relied upon by those who wanted to write about Sir Thomas, with no mention of Margaret's work to preserve her father's legacy for posterity. The laws against Catholicism brought in by Queen Elizabeth in 1558, and the accompanying anti-Catholic feeling in the country, continued well into the Victorian era. Catholicism only became legal in 1829, and then it took many years for it to be accepted widely.[12] As a result of this anti-Catholic feeling, and the lack of attention to Catholic scholarship due to it, the translations done by these women fell out of favour and were largely forgotten or lost. Sir Thomas's work alone appears to have been the one thing that kept on being studied and was, therefore, kept and preserved, but had it not been for Margaret's perseverance, this would not have been possible. She is overlooked as she was so keen to keep her father's name on the documentation, not her own.

Conclusion

Margaret's life was full of turmoil. She dealt with tribulation, change and religious tumult throughout her lifetime, and saw so many of her family members taken away, imprisoned, taken by illness or by the will of the king's axe, that when reading about her as a person, it is difficult to put yourself into her shoes. But, all through these challenges, she carried on with the threads that kept her focused; her faith, her family and her mind, and this is what makes Margaret special.

There were a number of examples of other women who were learned, or who received an education which made them unusual. Her own sisters were among this group of remarkable, women who experienced something atypical for the period, and these women all deserve a place in the history books, but Margaret stands out. Even in her own time, contemporaries singled her out as 'the most noble of any that lived in this world', and these accolades came from all over the western world. They came from people who were well known for their own scholarship, and who were greatly respected, and yet they had nothing but praise for her talents.[1] Her example was given in the context of books on the subject of educating children, given as a goal, as something for women to emulate and an example to consider as a good reason to encourage women and girls to learn and to grow. She was something of an icon for the humanist movement, and for her father's cause, both contemporarily and in the years that followed, and right up to the present day.

John Guy theorised that, in fact, Margaret was not able to achieve her full potential. This was not just because of her gender, or the setbacks that she had with regards to the laws, or her father's untimely death. He surmises that Margaret could well have been the key to helping the humanist Catholic cause. In the same way that Tyndale and others were writing pro-reformist works in Europe, had the humanist group, including her own father, seen her full potential, they would have been able to use her skills as a linguist and writer to put forward a popular and accessible competitor for Tyndale. As Guy puts so eloquently:

The tragedy, from the official church's viewpoint, is that Tyndale lacked competition. The church authorities were unable to see that the one person in England that knew Latin and Greek to the point where she could correct Erasmus, who could match Tyndale as a translator and stylist, and could be relied on to conform to the Catholic teaching and doctrine, was Margaret Roper.[2]

As events unfolded through the sixteenth century, her influence was muted due to the changing religious tones in England, but that does not mean that Margaret's influence, and that of the others included with her, cannot be seen at all. Women's education did increase and improve in the generations immediately following her childhood and that of her own children, and it did in effect plateau, rather than regress back to a one-dimensional view of a woman's place being purely as a home-maker. Reading became commonplace, and the ability to read and to learn became a core of what made a 'good' woman, able to read scriptures, learn about the world, teach her children and to lead a good Christian life. Women were also able to publish works in their own names, something that prior to Margaret's publication of *Devout Treatise* had not been seen as possible for non-royal women. This can be seen continuing throughout the centuries, and even up to the mid-nineteenth century, when education for all began to be seen as the way ahead, regardless of wealth, status or gender.

Perhaps the only issue we really have is being able to see what was, in the words of Peter Kaufman, 'Absolute Margaret'.[3] Most of what we know about Margaret comes from the men around her: from the writings of her father, of those who were her friends and allies, her husband or even just men who were familiar with her reputation. We therefore have to work hard to know her properly, and to see who she really was and to try to hear what Margaret thought, believed or stood for. In the preface to his biography of Margaret, E.E. Reynolds starts by saying:

> It is not possible to write a year-by-year biography of Margaret Roper as the materials we have are so unevenly distributed over the forty years of her life. This defect in the records may explain why no one has attempted hitherto to give an account of her life. It may also be that she stood so near her father that he has overshadowed her, and it has been difficult to think of her as a personality in her own right.[4]

This is the problem that many have had with attempting to piece together Margaret as a whole person. As with many early modern women all we have are fleeting glances at their lives and very little about their personalities. However, thanks to Margaret herself and those around her, we do have something more to offer about her in particular, and as a result we may also shine a brighter light on the lives of early modern women in general. Early modern women are often left out of the narrative, and are not given credit for forming it. As we see from Sir Thomas's letters, the More women were a strong bunch, and with Dame Alice as a role model this is hardly surprising. They ran the households, took on charity work, educated children, did translations and scholarly work for pleasure, learned musical instruments, entertained diplomats, exchanged letters with well-known scholars, and all while maintaining the expectations of what an early modern woman should be. While it is clear that the More women, Dame Alice, Margaret and her sisters, were far from the average, their experiences and the events of their lives give us an insight into how other households would have been run, and perhaps how other women would have responded to similar scenarios.

We do, however, have a wide range of descriptions, or opinions and of correspondence with Margaret in particular to know more about her than we do about her sisters, and many other women. The portraits by Holbein, combined with Erasmus's statement that the likenesses are true, suggest that the images we have of Sir Thomas and his family are accurate, and this is helpful in visualising the family, and Margaret as an individual. It also gives us some evidence to suggest that Holbein's other portraits in general were accurate, which is useful to know when using them to study an individual. The letters we have from her father, addressed to her and her siblings, give us a window into everyday life in the household, and households like theirs, and also the relationships between a father and his children and vice versa.

Without Sir Thomas's letters, we may not have as much information about the English court, and events leading up to his execution that were so important in the history of England. The court and council records for the period no longer exist, and so without accounts such as that of Sir Thomas, we would be without crucial evidence about events, and while his accounts are obviously just one point of view, they are so detailed and so well written (thanks to his skill as a wordsmith), historians today are still using them to aid their studies.

It is also not simply a scholarly interest that is helped by Margaret's passion for her father's legacy. On 19 May 1935, Sir Thomas More was canonised by the pope in recognition of his loyalty to the Catholic faith that led to his martyrdom. The following of St Thomas More is popular all over the world, with pilgrims making the trip to see sites associated with him, including the Roper Chapel in Canterbury where his head is most probably interred. His story has inspired a huge number of works of art and books examining his life and what he stood for. Thanks to the many portraits, letters and documents we have that belonged to him, people are able to get to know the man that was Sir Thomas More in great detail. What is interesting is that a lot of these artworks also include Margaret; they commemorate their times together in the Tower, such as *Sir Thomas More and his Daughter* by John Rogers Herbert (1844), or when she ran through the guards to kiss him when he was sentenced to death.[5] There is even a famous painting of her rescuing his head from Tower Bridge, painted in 1873 by Lucy Madox Brown.[6]

A number of these portraits were painted after the relaxation of the anti-Catholic laws in the mid-nineteenth century, and this shows just how much the legacy of Sir Thomas More, and therefore of Margaret, had endured.

The interest in them both continues today, as they form a key part of the story of the Tudor era and dynasty. Literature, cinema and television have all shown the role played by Sir Thomas More, and often show 'Meg' right there next to him. In *A Man for All Seasons* (1966), we get to see the whole More family brought vividly to life as we follow Sir Thomas through his final years and up to his execution. More modern dramas such as *The Tudors* and *Wolf Hall*, based on the books by Hilary Mantel, have Sir Thomas and his family as supporting players in the story that was the reign of Henry VIII. For all these dramas, while the conversations may be entirely fictional, an enormous amount of research is undertaken to ensure they are as accurate as possible; this usually stems from the original documents.

All the information required by historians, artists and writers would not be available were it not for Margaret's own determination to preserve the documents that contain it. In her actions, she not only preserved her father, but she preserved herself for future generations, and allowed us to see into her remarkable life. Margaret's importance cannot and should not be understated. She, along with others of her generation, paved the way for women to read, write and make an impact. While they maybe did not do this ostentatiously, or while claiming credit for their work, their contribution can be found just below the surface or by reading between the lines.

Margaret in particular though can truly be shown to have made a contribution to the study of history. By working to preserve the story of her father and the scholarship he produced, Margaret and those that followed her example, kept a vital source of information to enable us to study and gain insight into the world of the More family, the reformation and the Tudor court.

Appendices

Appendix 1: The More Family

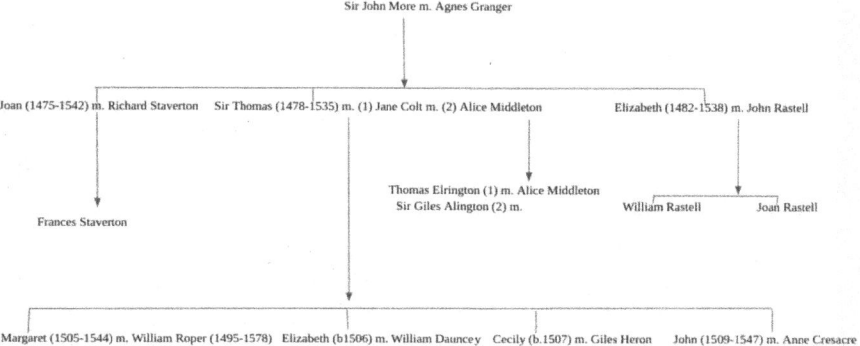

Appendix 2: The Children of Margaret More and William Roper

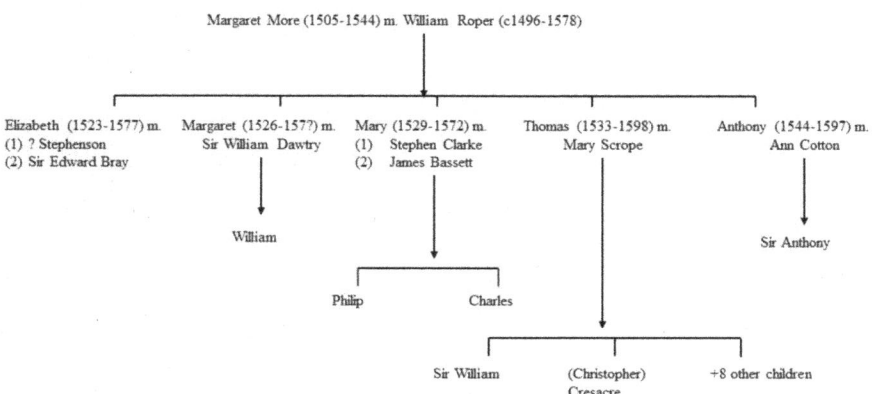

Bibliography

Primary Sources

Ascham, Roger, and Alvin Vos, *Letters of Roger Ascham* (1989).

Ascham, Roger, *The Scholemaster* (1570), reprinted by A. Constable and Company, 1870.

Caius, John, *A Boke or Counseill Against the Disease Commonly Called the Sweate, or Sweatyng Sicknesse* (1552).

Foxe, John, *Foxe's Book of Martyrs: Select Narratives* (1563), reprinted by OUP Oxford, 2009.

Hall, Edward, *Hall's Chronicle: Containing the History of England, During the Reign of Henry the Fourth, and the Succeeding Monarchs, to the end of the Reign Of Henry the Eighth, in Which are Particularly Described the Manners and Customs of Those Periods. Carefully Collated with the Editions of 1548 And 1550*, J. Johnson, London, 1809, pp.507–509.

Howell, T.B., *Complete Collection of State Trials and Proceeding Upon Impeachments for High Treason, etc.* (London, 1719).

Le Forestier, Thomas, *Tractatus contra pestilentiam, thenasmonem et dissinteriam*, Guillaume le Talleur (1490).

More, Thomas, *The Coronation Ode the King Henry VIII and Queen Catherine*, 1509, https://thomasmorestudies.org/wp-content/uploads/2020/08/Mores_1509_Coronation_Ode.pdf

More, Thomas, *Response to Luther*, 1523, www.reverendluther.org/pdfs2/Thomas-More-Response-to-Luther.pdf

More, Thomas, *A Dialogue Concerning Heresies*, 1530, https://thomasmorestudies.org/wp-content/uploads/2020/09/DialogueConcerningHeresies2015-etext.pdf

More, Thomas, *The Last Letters of Thomas More*, edited by Alvaro De Silva, Eerdmans Publishing (2000).

More, Saint Thomas, and Elizabeth Frances Rogers, *The Correspondence of St Thomas More* (Ed. 1947).

Roper, Margaret, *A Devout Treatise upon the Paternoster* (1524). A translation of the original work by Erasmus, https://quod.lib.umich.edu/e/eebo/A00361.0001.001/1:1?rgn=div1;view=fulltext

Roper, Margaret, *Letter to Alice Alington from Margaret Roper* (August 1534), http://law2.umkc.edu/faculty/projects/ftrials/more/alington1534.html

Roper, William, Thomas More, and Alfred L. Rowse, *A Man of Singular Virtue*. London: The Folio Society (1980).

Stapleton, Thomas, and Philip Edward Hallett, *The Life and Illustrious Martyrdom of Sir Thomas More*. London: Burns & Oates (1966).

Stow, John, *A survey of London*. Whittaker and Company (1842).

Vives, Juan Luis, *The Education of a Christian Woman: A Sixteenth-Century Manual*. University of Chicago Press (2000).

Secondary Sources

Ackroyd, Peter, *The Life of Thomas More*. Anchor (2012).

Aughterson, Kate, ed., *Renaissance Woman: A Sourcebook: Constructions of Femininity In England*. Taylor & Francis US (1995).

Benson, Pamela Joseph, *Invention of the Renaissance Woman: The Challenge of Female Independence in the Literature and Thought of Italy and England*. Penn State Press (2010).

Berthold, Cornelius, and Claudia Colini, '"The most noble of any that ever lived in this world": an encrypted text praising Thomas More's daughter Margaret, contained in a miniature Qur'an at the Bodleian Libraries.' *Moreana* 60, No. 1 (2023), pp.95–113.

Best, Michael, *The Age of Marriage: Life and Times*, https://internetshakespeare.uvic.ca/Library/SLT/society/family/marriage.html

Campbell, William Edward, *Erasmus, Tyndale and More*. Eyre & Spottiswoode (1949).

Cousins, A.D., 'Humanism, Female Education, and Myth: Erasmus, Vives, and More's "To Candidus"'. *Journal of the History of Ideas* 65, No. 2 (2004), pp.213–30. www.jstor.org/stable/3654207.

Crowther, David, *Mountjoy, Henry VIII's Humanist Mentor – The History of England*, https://thehistoryofengland.co.uk/resource/mountjoy-henry-viiis-humanist-mentor/

Davenport, Cyril, *Thomas Berthelet, Royal Printer and Bookbinder to Henry VIII ... With Special Reference to his Bookbindings*. Chicago: Caxton Club (1901).

Demers, Patricia, *Women's Writing in English: Early Modern England*. University of Toronto Press (2005).

Dowling, Maria, '*Humanism in the Age of Henry VIII*' (1986).

Gee, Henry and Hardy, William (ed.), *Documents Illustrative of English Church History*. London: Macmillan (1914).

Goldberg, Jonathan, *Desiring Women Writing: English Renaissance Examples*. Stanford University Press (1997).

Goodrich, Jaime, *Faithful Translators: Authorship, Gender, and Religion in Early Modern England*. Northwestern University Press (2013).

Goodrich, Jaime, 'Thomas More and Margaret More Roper: A Case for Rethinking Women's Participation in the Early Modern Public Sphere'. *The Sixteenth Century Journal* 39, no. 4 (2008), pp.1021–40, https://doi.org/10.2307/20479136.

Guy, John, *A Daughter's Love: Thomas and Margaret More – The Family Who Dared to Defy Henry VIII*. Penguin UK (2012).

Guy, J.A., *Tudor England*. Oxford (1990).

Guy, J.A., 'Henry VIII and the Praemunire Manoeuvres of 1530–1531'. *The English Historical Review* 97, no. 384 (1982), pp.481–503, www.jstor.org/stable/570060.

Haselkorn, Anne M., and Betty Travitsky, *The Renaissance Englishwoman in Print: Counterbalancing the Canon*. University of Massachusetts Press (1990).

Heyman P., Simons L., Cochez C., 'Were the English Sweating Sickness and The Picardy Sweat Caused by Hantaviruses?' *Viruses*. 2014 Jan 7;6(1), pp.151–71, Doi: 10.3390/v6010151; PMID: 24402305; PMCID: PMC3917436.

Ives, Eric, *The Life and Death of Anne Boleyn: 'The Most Happy'*. Blackwell (2004).

Kaufman, Gloria, 'Juan Luis Vives on the education of women'. *Signs: Journal of Women in Culture and Society* 3, no. 4 (1978), pp.891–6.

Kaufman, Peter Iver, 'Absolute Margaret: Margaret More Roper and "Well Learned" Men'. *The Sixteenth Century Journal* 20, no. 3 (1989), pp.443–56.

Khanna, Lee Cullen, *Early Tudor Translators: Margaret Beaufort, Margaret More Roper and Mary Basset*. Aldershot: Ashgate (2001).
Knowles, David, 'The Religious Orders in England – 3 The Tudor Age'. *The Religious Orders in England* (1959).
Lamb, Mary Ellen, 'Margaret Roper, the Humanist Political Project, and the Problem of Agency'. In *Ashgate Critical Essays on Women Writers in England, 1550–1700*, pp.95–120. Routledge (2017).
Linder, D.O., *The Trial of Sir Thomas More Knight, Lord Chancellor of England, for High Treason in denying; the King's Supremacy, May 7, 1535. the 26th of Henry VIII*, https://famous-trials.com/thomasmore/997-moretrialreport
Luders, A. and others, eds., *Statutes of the Realm*, 11 vols. in 12, RC (1810–1828), vol. 3, pp.446–51.
Marius, Richard, *Thomas More: A Biography*, Harvard University Press (1999).
McCutcheon, Elizabeth, 'Decoding the Alice Alington-Margaret More Roper Letters', *Moreana* 57, no. 2 (2020), pp.144–70.
McCutcheon, Elizabeth, and Katharina Wilson, 'Margaret More Roper'. *Women Writers of the Renaissance and Reformation*, ed. Katharina Wilson (1987), pp.449–80.
More, Cresacre, '*The life and death of Sir Thomas Moore Lord high Chancellour of England*', English recusant literature 66 (1971).
O'Day, Rosemary, *Education and Society 1500–1800: The Social Foundations of Education in Early Modern Britain* (1982).
Olivares-Merino, Eugenio M., 'A month with the Mores: The meeting of Juan Luis Vives and Margaret More Roper'. *English Studies* 88, no. 4 (2007), pp.388–400.
Payne, Linda, 'Health in England (16th–18th c.)', in *Children and Youth in History*, Item #166, https://cyh.rrchnm.org/items/show/166
Pope, Charles, 'The Lost Liturgies File: The Churching of Women', https://blog.adw.org/2010/02/lost-liturgies-file-the-churching-of-women/
Rabil Jr, Albert, ed., *Renaissance Humanism, Volume 1: Foundations, Forms, and Legacy*. Vol. 1, University of Pennsylvania Press (2016).
Reynolds, Ernest Edwin, *Margaret Roper: Eldest Daughter of St Thomas More*. London: Burns and Oates (1960).
Sim, Alison, *The Tudor Housewife*, The History Press (2010).
Sowards, J. Kelley, 'Erasmus and the Education of Women'. *The Sixteenth Century Journal* (1982), pp.77–89.

Summit, Jennifer, *Lost Property: The Woman Writer and English Literary History, 1380–1589*. University of Chicago Press (2000).

Taylor, Andrew, 'How to Hold Your Tongue: John Christopherson's Plutarch and the Mid-Tudor Politics of Catholic Humanism'. *Canadian Review of Comparative Literature* 41, no. 4 (2014), pp.411–31, Doi:10.1353/crc.2014.0038.

ThoughtCo., '*Recite This Prayer for a Deceased Mother*'. Learn Religions, www.learnreligions.com/prayer-for-a-deceased-mother-542702

Urquhart, Francis Fortescue, 'William Roper'. In Herbermann, Charles (ed.), *Catholic Encyclopedia*, Vol. 13. New York: Robert Appleton Company (1912).

Wilcox, Helen, ed., *Women and Literature in Britain, 1500–1700*, Vol. 17, Cambridge University Press (1996).

Wagner, John A., and Susan Walters Schmid, *Encyclopedia of Tudor England [3 volumes]*, ABC-CLIO (2011).

Woolfson, Jonathan, ed., *Reassessing Tudor Humanism*. Springer (2002).

Yielding, Cheryl E., 'Emancipation & Renewal: English Catholicism in the Nineteenth Century', (1982). Master of Arts (MA), Thesis, History, Old Dominion University, DOI: 10.25777/vgjz-9x15, https://digitalcommons.odu.edu/

Endnotes

Preface

1. Reynolds, Ernest Edwin, *Margaret Roper. Eldest Daughter of St Thomas More*, London: Burns and Oates (1960), Preface.

Introduction

1. Sources vary on the name of Thomas More's first wife. She is referred to as Jane, Joan, Joanne and Joanna by various sources. However, the inscription on the tomb in Chelsea Old Church, refers to her as 'Johannas' or Joanna. Therefore, I have chosen to use Joanna throughout this book.
2. Reynolds, p.2.
3. Roper, William, Thomas More and Alfred L. Rowse, *A Man of Singular Virtue*, London: The Folio Society (1980), p.28, *Marriage*.
4. Reynolds, p.6.
5. Sim, Alison, *The Tudor Housewife*, The History Press (2010), pp.9–10.
6. Ackroyd, Peter, *The Life of Thomas More* Anchor (2012), p.4.
7. Survey of London by John Stow, published 1598.
8. Appendix 1: The More Family Tree.
9. Ackroyd, p.116.
10. Ibid.
11. Image 1: Norden's Map of London *c.*1593 shows the position of Bucklersbury, Cheapside and other major landmarks.
12. Lynda Payne, 'Health in England (16th–18th c.)', in *Children and Youth in History*, Item #166, https://cyh.rrchnm.org/items/show/166.

Chapter One

1. Hall, Edward, *Hall's Chronicle: Containing the History of England ... to the End of the Reign of Henry the Eighth ... Carefully Collated with the Editions of 1548 and 1550*, J. Johnson, London (1809), pp.507–509.

2. *The Coronation Ode the King Henry VIII and Queen Catherine* by Thomas More (1509), https://thomasmorestudies.org/wp-content/uploads/2020/08/Mores_1509_Coronation_Ode.pdf
3. Guy, John, *A Daughter's Love: Thomas and Margaret More – The Family Who Dared to Defy Henry VIII.* Penguin UK (2012), p.13.
4. Sim, p.31.
5. Guy, *A Daughter's Love*, p.16.
6. Ibid, p.17.
7. Ibid, p.37.
8. Caius, John, *A Boke or Counseill Against the Disease Commonly Called the Sweate, or Sweatyng Sicknesse* (1552).
9. Heyman P., Simons L., Cochez C., 'Were the English Sweating Sickness and The Picardy Sweat Caused by Hantaviruses?', *Viruses*, 2014 Jan 7;6(1), pp.151–71, Doi: 10.3390/v6010151; PMID: 24402305; PMCID: PMC3917436.
10. Le Forestier, Thomas, *Tractatus contra pestilentiam, thenasmonem et dissinteriam.* Guillaume le Talleur (1490).
11. The theory about Joanna's death due to childbirth complications is explored by E.E. Reynolds (*Margaret Roper*, p.8) and is mentioned by Ackroyd as a potential explanation for her death.
12. Example of a Catholic prayer for the loss of a mother taken from www.learnreligions.com/prayer-for-a-deceased-mother-542702
13. Ackroyd, p.138.
14. Guy, *A Daughter's Love*, p.39.
15. John Bouge's account taken from Guy referenced as National Archives, Kew, SP 1/239, fos. 223–4; J. Gairdner (1892).
16. Reynolds, p.9.
17. The quote about 'going against friends' advice', comes from Wagner, John A., and Susan Walters Schmid. *Encyclopedia of Tudor England [3 volumes].* ABC-CLIO, 2011.
18. Reynolds, p.10.
19. Guy, *A Daughter's Love*, p.31.
20. Reynolds, p.7.
21. Inscription from the tomb at Chelsea Old Church. Translation from Reynolds, p.8.
22. Guy, *A Daughter's Love*, p.55.

Chapter Two

1. Guy, *A Daughter's Love*, p.15.
2. Reynolds, p.14.
3. Guy, *A Daughter's Love*, p.145.
4. Ackroyd, p.137.
5. Description of everyday life taken from information in Guy, *A Daughter's Love*, and Ackroyd, *The Life of Thomas More*.
6. https://thehistoryofengland.co.uk/resource/mountjoy-henry-viiis-humanist-mentor (accessed 5 June 2023).
7. Ibid.
8. Ackroyd, p.80.
9. Guy, *A Daughter's Love*, p.31.
10. Ibid.
11. Quote from a letter from Erasmus to Thomas More in 1509, explaining his reasons behind the writing of 'Moraie Encomium' and his admiration of Thomas.
12. Guy, *A Daughter's Love*, p.31.
13. Ibid., p.36.
14. Ibid.

Chapter Three

1. Sim, p.31.
2. Ibid., p.39.
3. Ackroyd, p.17.
4. Roper, *A Man of Singular Virtue*, pp.27–8.
5. Sim, p.34.
6. Aughterson, Kate, ed. *Renaissance Woman: A Sourcebook: Constructions of Femininity in England*. Taylor & Francis US (1995), p.167.
7. Sim, p.36, quoting from Bullinger's '*The Christen State of Matrimonye*' (1541).
8. Ives, Eric, *The Life and Death of Anne Boleyn: 'The Most Happy'*, Blackwell (2004), pp.18–20.
9. Reynolds, p.6, quoting Erasmus's letter of 1519.
10. Reynolds, p.9.
11. Warnicke, Retha, 'Women and Humanism in England', in Rabil Jr, Albert, ed. *Renaissance Humanism*, Volume 1: Foundations, Forms, and Legacy, University of Pennsylvania Press (2016), p.40.

12. Benson, Pamela Joseph, *Invention of the Renaissance Woman: The Challenge of Female Independence in the Literature and Thought of Italy and England*. Penn State Press (2010), p.158.
13. Warnicke, p.42.
14. Kaufman, Gloria, 'Juan Luis Vives on the education of women'. *Signs: Journal of Women in Culture and Society* 3, no. 4 (1978), pp.891–6.
15. Stapleton, Thomas, *The Life and Illustrious Martyrdom of Sir Thomas More*. London: Burns & Oates (1966), p.91.
16. Reynolds, p.12, quoting from Roper, *A Man of Singular Virtue*.
17. Reynolds, p.21.
18. Stapleton, p.91.
19. Reynolds, pp.13–14.
20. Reynolds, p.15, quoting from the Letter from Thomas More to William Gonnell.
21. Reynolds, p.17.
22. Ibid., p.23.
23. Reynolds, p.26 – quote from Juan Luis Vives, *Instruction of a Christian Woman*, translated into English by Richard Hyrde at the suggestion of Thomas More.
24. Reynolds, p.24 – 'Letter from Thomas More to his Dearest Children and to Margaret Giggs whom he numbers among his own'.
25. Reynolds, p.21 – Extract of a letter from Thomas More to his daughter Margaret, given in full in Stapleton's biography. In the letter, the 'Shaw' referenced is most probably one of the servants attached to the More household.
26. Reynolds, p.24 – '*Letter to my Dearest Children*' by Thomas More.
27. Reynolds, p.28.
28. Ibid.

Chapter Four

1. https://internetshakespeare.uvic.ca/Library/SLT/society/family/marriage.html (accessed 27 May 2023).
2. Urquhart, Francis Fortescue, 'William Roper'. In Herbermann, Charles (ed.), *Catholic Encyclopedia*, Vol. 13, New York: Robert Appleton Company (1912).
3. Appendix 1: The More Family.

4. Ackroyd, p.213.
5. Image 3: Later picture of More's house at Chelsea when it was Beaufort House.
6. Roper, p.47.
7. Reynolds, p.46, quoting Erasmus's letter to John Faber, Bishop of Vienna.
8. Reynolds, p.28, quoting a letter from February 1521.
9. Image 4: Picture of the front cover of Devout Treatise from British Library. Text taken from Early English Books Online (EEBO) : https://quod.lib.umich.edu/e/eebo/A00361.0001.001/1:1?rgn=div1;view=fulltext
10. *Early Tudor Translators : Margaret Beaufort, Margaret More Roper, and Mary Basset*, selected and introduced by Lee Cullen Khanna.
11. Goodrich, Jaime, *Faithful Translators: Authorship, Gender, and Religion in Early Modern England*. Northwestern University Press (2013), p.29.
12. Ibid., p.31.
13. Image 4: Front cover of *Devout Treatise upon the Paternoster*.
14. Reynolds, p.25.
15. Guy, *A Daughter's Love*, p.157.
16. Goodrich, p.31.
17. Devout Treatise on EEBO.
18. Ibid.
19. Guy, *A Daughter's Love*, p.150.
20. Information about Thomas Berthelet from: Cyril Davenport (1901), Thomas Berthelet, Royal Printer and Bookbinder to Henry VIII … With Special Reference to his Bookbindings.
21. Appendix 1: The More Family Tree.
22. Hyrde's introduction – *Devout Treatise* on EEBO.
23. Guy, *A Daughter's Love*, p.157.
24. An image of this page is included in the copies shown in: *Early Tudor Translators: Margaret Beaufort, Margaret More Roper, and Mary Basset*, selected and introduced by Lee Cullen Khanna.

Chapter Five

1. Sim, p.17.
2. www.tudorsociety.com/childbirth-in-medieval-and-tudor-times-by-sarah-bryson/ (accessed 5 February 2023).

3. Ibid.
4. Sim, p.22.
5. Ibid., p.18.
6. Pope, Charles, 'The Lost Liturgies File: The Churching of Women', https://blog.adw.org/2010/02/lost-liturgies-file-the-churching-of-women/
7. In *A Daughter's Love,* John Guy speculates about Anthony being named for the *Dialogue of Comfort* character.
8. Reynolds, p.37.
9. Ibid.
10. Taylor, Andrew, 'How to Hold Your Tongue: John Christopherson's Plutarch and the Mid-Tudor Politics of Catholic Humanism'. *Canadian Review of Comparative Literature* 41, no. 4 (2014), pp.411–31.
11. Roper, p.66.
12. Guy, *A Daughter's Love*, p.155.
13. Ibid., p.156.
14. Ibid., p.164.
15. Ibid.

Chapter Six

1. Roper, pp.46–7.
2. Reynolds, p.46.
3. Translation of coded message taken from: Berthold, Cornelius, and Claudia Colini. '"The most noble of any that ever lived in this world": an encrypted text praising Thomas More's daughter Margaret, contained in a miniature Qur'an at the Bodleian Libraries'. *Moreana* 60, no. 1 (2023), pp.5–113.
4. Ibid.
5. Roper, pp.49–50.
6. Reynolds, pp.56–7.
7. Ibid, p.53.
8. Image 5: Holbein portrait of the More Family.
9. Letter from Erasmus to Margaret Roper quoted in Reynolds pp.53–4.
10. Translation of the letter written by Margaret Roper to Erasmus *c.* October 1529. The original is located in the archives of the University of Wroclaw, Poland. A holograph image is included in Reynolds, p.54, and an image can be seen in Image 6.

11. *A Dialogue Concerning Heresies* accessed via https://thomasmorestudies. org/wp-content/uploads/2020/09/DialogueConcerningHeresies2015-etext.pdf
12. Ackroyd, p.271.
13. Ibid.
14. Marius, Richard, *Thomas More: A Biography*, Harvard University Press (1999), p.404.

Chapter Seven

1. Guy, J.A., 'Henry VIII and the Praemunire Manoeuvres of 1530–1531'. *The English Historical Review* 97, no. 384 (1982), pp.481–503, www.jstor.org/stable/570060.
2. Roper, p.66.
3. Ibid., p.68.
4. Ibid.
5. Images 7 & 8: Miniature Holbein portraits of William and Margaret *c*.1532.
6. Roper, pp.69–70. Sir Thomas's response to the Bishops regarding non-attendance at the coronation of Queen Anne.
7. Luders, A. and others, eds., *Statutes of The Realm*, 11 vols. in 12, RC (1810–1828), Vol. 3, pp.446–51, (25 Henry VIII, *c*.12, Statutes of the Realm, p.446).
8. Ackroyd, p.341.
9. Ibid., p.358.
10. https://thomasmorestudies.org/wp-content/uploads/2020/09/EnglishCorrespondence-etext.pdf, p.89.
11. Oath of Supremacy 1535 found in full: https://queenanneboleyn.com/2012/02/25/oath-of-supremacy-1535-actual-text-sir-thomas-audley/
12. Oath of Succession 1534 found in full: https://queenanneboleyn.com/2012/02/25/oath-of-succession-1534-actual-text-sir-thomas-audley/

Chapter Eight

1. Guy, *A Daughter's Love*, p.233.
2. Roper, p.121.

3. Guy in *A Daughter's Love* theorises 'She therefore sent him a letter, folded but unsealed, knowing it would be intercepted by Cromwell'.
4. Guy, *A Daughter's Love*, p.236.
5. Roper, p.84.
6. Ackroyd, p.369, An extract of a letter by Lady Alice More.
7. Ackroyd, p.370.
8. From *The Last Letters of Thomas More*, edited by Alvaro De Silva, (Eerdmans Publishing, 2000, pp.72–89). http://law2.umkc.edu/faculty/projects/ftrials/more/alington1534.html
9. Ibid.
10. Treason Act quoted from: *Documents Illustrative of English Church History*, edited by Henry Gee and William John Hardy, London: Macmillan (1914).
11. *Complete Collection of State Trials and Proceeding Upon Impeachments for High Treason, etc.*, London (1719).
12. Ibid.
13. Ibid.
14. Roper, pp.92–3.
15. This is the sequence of events as laid out in Guy, *A Daughter's Love*, pp.262–3.
16. Guy, *A Daughter's Love*, pp.263–4.
17. Ibid., p.266.

Chapter Nine

1. Stapleton, p.191.
2. Ibid, p.193.
3. Knowles, David, 'The religious orders in England/3 The Tudor age'. *The Religious Orders in England* (1959), pp.235–6.
4. Guy, *A Daughter's Love*, p.234.
5. Guy, *A Daughter's Love*, p.267, quoting from Cresacre More's 'The life and death of Sir Thomas Moore Lord high Chancellour of England' (1631).
6. What remains of the buildings of Well Hall in Eltham is now used as a restaurant, www.tudorbarneltham.com/
7. Image 9: The Roper Gate in Canterbury.
8. Guy, *Tudor England* (1990), p.195.
9. Ascham, Roger, and Alvin Vos, *Letters of Roger Ascham* (1989), p.250.

10. Guy, *A Daughter's Love*, p.267.
11. Ibid., p.268.
12. Ibid.
13. Ibid., p.270.
14. In the notes for the chapter including Margaret's death, Guy references a 'Plague epidemic' in London and Westminster, *A Daughter's Love*, p.326.
15. Durrant, Catherine Sidney, *A Link between Flemish Mystics and English Martyrs* (Benziger, 1925), pp.184–6.

Chapter Ten

1. Introduction to Roper, by A.L. Rowse, p.10.
2. Images 10 & 11: The exterior and interior of the Roper Chapel at St Dunstan's Church, Canterbury.
3. Somner's *Antiquities of Canterbury*, accessed through: https://quod.lib.umich.edu/e/eebo/A12598.0001.001/1:32.8.32?rgn=div3;view=fulltext, p.342. The original inscription on William and Margaret's tomb is in Latin, and here I have translated to English.
4. Goodrich, Chapter 1: 'Private Spheres'.
5. Khanna, Lee Cullen, *Early Tudor Translators: Margaret Beaufort, Margaret More Roper and Mary Basset*. Aldershot: Ashgate (2001).
6. Ibid.
7. Letter from Jesuit priest Robert Persons, recommending Charles Basset for a position at the English College in Rome.
8. Haselkorn, Anne M., and Betty Travitsky, *The Renaissance Englishwoman in Print: Counterbalancing the Canon*. University of Massachusetts Press (1990), p.11.
9. Ascham, Roger, and Judith Boss, *The Scholemaster (1570)*, R.S. Bear, 1998.
10. Ibid.
11. Statistics about literacy rates for England taken from: https://blogs.qub.ac.uk/medievalforum/2015/08/19/literacy-and-print-in-early-modern-germany-and-england/ (accessed 17 April 2023).
12. Yielding, Cheryl E., 'Emancipation & Renewal: English Catholicism in the Nineteenth Century' (1982). Master of Arts (MA), Thesis, History, Old Dominion University, DOI: 10.25777/vgjz-9x15

Conclusion

1. Berthold, *Moreana*, Vol. 60, Issue 1, pp.95–113.
2. Guy, *A Daughter's Love*, p.159.
3. Kaufman, Peter Iver, 'Absolute Margaret: Margaret More Roper and "Well Learned" Men'. *The Sixteenth Century Journal* 20, no. 3 (1989), pp.443–56.
4. Reynolds, Preface.
5. Image 13: John Rogers Herbert, *Sir Thomas More and his Daughter*, 1844.
6. Image 14: Lucy Madox Brown, *Margaret Roper Rescuing the Head of her Father*, 1880.

Index

Aesop's Fables, 5
Allington Letters, 123–4
Allington, Alice (née Middleton), xvii–xviii, 29, 50, 76, 123
Ammonio, Andrea, 12–13, 19, 26–7
Ascham, Roger, 44, 141–3, 154

Baptism, 72–3
Barton, Elizabeth, 110–11
Bassett, Mary (née Roper), 74, 78, 151–2
Beaufort, Margaret, 58
Berthelet, Thomas, 64, 67
Blount, William, 22
Boleyn, Anne, 101–102, 107–108, 111, 137, 139
Bray, Elizabeth (née Roper), 71, 74
Bucklersbury, xvii, 1, 121
Butts Close, 54, 77, 121

Catherine of Aragon, xviii, 37, 68, 87, 101, 104, 107
Cheapside, xvi, 1
Chelsea, 54, 77, 106
Chelsea Old Church, 14, 56, 78, 145, 149
Childbirth, 71
Childhood, 4, 29–30
Christmas, 14, 26
Christopherson, John, 78, 141

Church of England, 102
Churching, 73
Clement, John, 40, 52, 121–2, 144
Coronation of Henry VIII, 1–2
Cramner, Thomas, 107, 144
Cromwell, Thomas, 110, 118, 126, 136

Dauncey, Elizabeth (née More), xviii, 52, 76
Dauncey, William, 18, 52, 76, 144
Dawtry, Margaret (née Roper), 74

Education, 30–2
Edward VI, xv
Elizabeth of York, xii, 22
Elrington, Thomas, 18, 50, 76
Eltham, Kent, 51, 69, 106
Eltham Palace, 22
Erasmus, Desiderius:
　correspondence with More family, 47, 75, 89, 93
　meets Prince Henry, 22
　relationship with Thomas More, 18–19, 21, 24, 26, 60
　writings, 24, 57, 61

Fisher, Bishop John, 103–104, 110, 112, 122, 136, 138
Funerals, 8–9

Gardiner, Stephen, 67
Giggs, Margaret, 16, 29, 38, 42, 52, 121, 133, 137, 145
Gonnell, William, 40–1
Great Yarmouth, xvii

Henry VII, xii, 1, 22
Henry VIII, xviii, 1, 22, 54, 78, 79–80, 87, 101, 103, 137
Heron, Giles, 18, 52, 76, 143
Heron, Cecily (née More), xviii, 52, 76, 143
Holbein, Hans, 91–2, 106, 161
Humanism, 21, 56, 52, 97
Hyrde, Richard, 37, 40, 56–7, 67

Infant Mortality, xviii

Kratzer, Nicholas, 40

Lincoln's Inn, xvi, 18, 22

Mary I, 37, 44, 78, 151–2
Midwives, 72
More, Anne (née Cresacre), 17, 52, 85
More, Dame Alice (previously Middleton):
　and Thomas More in the Tower, 119–20
　children, 11
　first marriage, 10
　marriage to Thomas More, 10–12, 29, 76, 85
　widowhood, 134, 139
More, Cresacre, 138, 148
More, Joanna (née Colt):
　and Erasmus, 26
　birth of children, xvii–xviii
　death, 6
　epitaph, 14
　funeral, 8–9
　marriage, xi–xv
　the Colts, xvii, 1
More, John, xviii, 46, 52, 144
More, Sir John, 1
More, Margaret:
　A Devout Treatise upon the Paternoster, 57, 61–64
　birth, xvii
　birth of children, 71, 74
　death, 145, 147
　letters to Erasmus, 95
　marriage, 51
　rescue of Father's head, 135
More, Sir Thomas:
　attitude to women, 35
　Chancellor, 83, 91, 97, 99, 101
　childhood, 30
　children, 5, 38–9, 46
　execution, 132
　hair shirt, 85
　in the Tower, 115, 117–19, 122
　Knight, 53
　marriage to Alice, 10
　marriage to Joanna, xi–xv
　MP, xvii, 1
　resignation, 103
　Speaker of the Commons, 53
　trial, 127–9
　Undersheriff, 3
　writings, 2, 4, 21, 36, 74, 79, 98, 100, 122

Netherhall, xiii

Oath of Succession, 114
Oath of Supremacy, 113

Pets, 5
Place Hall, 139
Pole, Reginald, 46, 56, 137
Pole, Geoffrey, 137
Praemunire, 107, 115
Pregnancy, 69–72
  Printing press, 64, 67

Rastell, Elizabeth (née More, sister of Sir Thomas), 72
Rastell, John, 64, 72
Rich, Sir Richard, 126–7
Roper, Anthony, 74, 144, 152
Role of Women, 33–5
Roper, Margaret, *see* More, Margaret
Roper, Thomas, 74
Roper, William:
  as an MP, 106
  background, 50
  comes to live with the Mores, 18, 51
  later life, 149
  marriage to Margaret, 51, 76
  protestantism, 80–1
  writings, 147–8

Roper Chapel, 149–50, 162
Roper Gate, 139
Roydon, Essex, xiii

Servants, 20
St Dunstan's Church, 69, 139
St Stephen's Church, xii, 8, 11, 51
Staverton, Frances, 65
Staverton, Joan (née More), xvi
Staverton, Richard, xvi
Stow, John, xvi
Sweating Sickness, 6–7

The Barge, xvii, 1, 8, 18, 21, 53
  inside, 3
  gardens, 5
The More School, 38, 65, 141, 155
The Tower of London, 115, 116, 132
Treason Act, 125

Vives, Juan-Luis, 36–37, 43, 68, 87, 154

Walbrook, xii, xvii
Warham, William, 91, 103, 107, 110
Weddings, xv, 49
Well Hall, 52, 139
Wolsey, Thomas, 17, 54, 67, 81, 99, 101
Wood, John, 21, 117